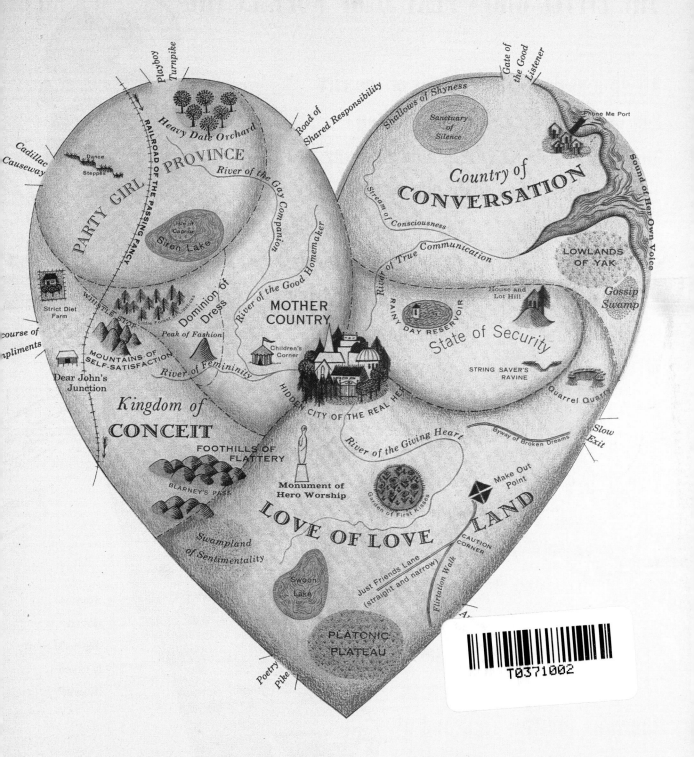

GEOGRAPHICAL GUIDE TO A
WOMAN'S HEART
emphasizing points of interest to the romantic traveler

Love

A Curious History in 50 Objects

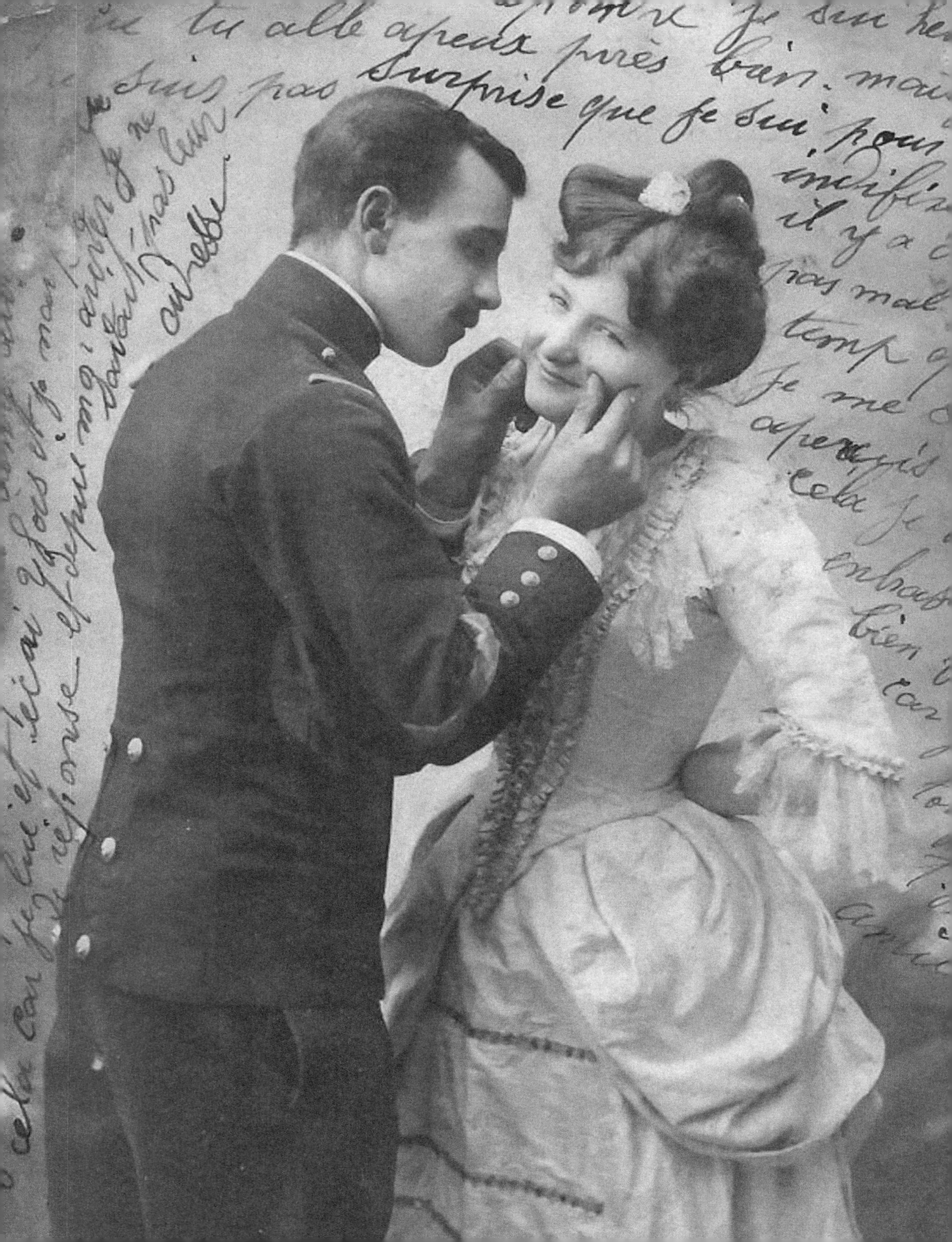

Love

A Curious History in 50 Objects

EDWARD
BROOKE-HITCHING

**SIMON &
SCHUSTER**

London · New York · Sydney · Toronto · New Delhi

MMXXIII

To Franklin and Emma

*Page 2: A French
lovers' postcard from c.1890.*

Opposite: Portrait of a Woman
with a Man at a Casement
by Filippo Lippi, c.1440.

Contents

Introduction

*'Love is a canvas furnished by nature
and embroidered by imagination.'*

Voltaire

The idea for this book was found in the armpits of nineteenth-century rural Austrian women. Specifically, with the slices of apple tucked *into* their armpits, as per tradition, as they danced away surrounded by a ring of young men watching with dread on their face. When the fruit was sufficiently soaked in sweat, the women would present it to their suitor of choice. If he was interested, he would consume the soggy slice with delight at being afforded the opportunity to share in her personal fragrance. If he declined, then back into the pit it went, ready for the next attempt.

In Fiji, a tradition is for the young man to present the father of his beloved with a whale's tooth, before asking for the hand of his daughter in marriage. The challenge with this is that the tooth has to be freshly wrenched from a living whale's mouth. Speaking of teeth, in traditional Hindu Balinese society, young men and women undergo a ritual tooth-filing ceremony, shaving down six of their teeth in order to advertise their arrival at marrying age.

Though these examples may seem a little extra in their challenge than more familiar customs, are they that much odder, philosophically speaking, than gifting a bouquet of severed plants in an attempt to woo? Perhaps it depends on how this is done, too. When the German multi-millionaire Gunter Sachs set out in May 1966 to win the heart of the most beautiful woman in the world, the French bombshell Brigitte Bardot, he did it with red roses – thousands of them, dropped by helicopter onto her Côte d'Azur property. 'It's not every day a man drops a ton of roses in your backyard,' Bardot later wrote in her autobiography, in a tone that almost suggests for her it wasn't every day *that week*.

From reading details like these it's impossible not to reflect on, and regret, how an ocean of love-driven stories and customs have been lost to time. In one sense love is ephemeral, invisible and impermanent (a 'smoke made with the fume of sighs', as Shakespeare so beautifully describes love in *Romeo and Juliet*); but to an historian love is an ancient engine of tumult and consequence. The idea for this book is to explore the role of love as a psychoactive agent of history and art by following the glittering material trail of curious objects, mysterious relics and inspired masterpieces left in its wake. Each item has a compelling and often unexpected story to tell, with the scale of the narratives swinging wildly from intimate relationships between just two historical figures in one chapter, to the philosophies, customs and love-and-lust deities (see pages 22-29) of entire cultures in another.

Opposite: Pair of Lovers *by the Master of the Housebook, c.1480-1485.*

But each provides windows into the relatable minds and emotional cores of people who lived thousands of years before us around the world.

For more than 5,000 years, poets, writers, artists and troubadours have broadcast the pleasures and the torments of love and lust – but we can go back even further to find love's footprints in the riverbed of time.

Love's Shadow (1867), *by Frederick Sandys, a dramatic painting of the darker side of love – envy, resentment, anger, perhaps even revenge – painted at a time when it was more common to find love idealised in paintings. Sandys originally planned to have his subject biting her own hair instead of the blue violets that the Victorian audience understood to symbolise love. Sandys would go on to marry the sitter, the actress Mary Emma Jones.*

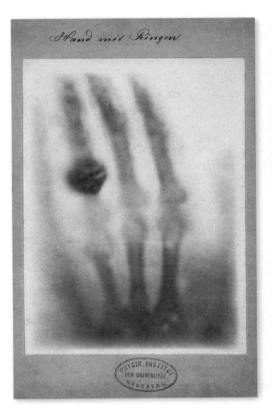

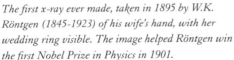

The first x-ray ever made, taken in 1895 by W.K. Röntgen (1845-1923) of his wife's hand, with her wedding ring visible. The image helped Röntgen win the first Nobel Prize in Physics in 1901.

The King of Love sits in a tree with two musicians, preparing to hurl his arrows at a couple sitting below. From the Maastricht Hours of the early fourteenth century.

The prehistoric carving known as the Ain Sakhri Lovers (see page 18), fashioned *c*.9000 BC, provides us with the oldest surviving depiction of a human embrace, while offering the excuse to attempt to track down the oldest kiss in (pre)history with – fair warning – slightly unsettling results. An introduction to love in ancient Mesopotamia is made by the goddess Inanna and Dumuzid, her doomed spouse with a wandering eye; while Egypt is represented by the chief royal scribe Yuny and his wife Renenutet, in a remarkable memorial carving of the couple that radiates such unusually relaxed and relatable intimacy that the distance of nearly 3,300 years between their lives and ours simply disappears.

With ancient Greece we find tragedy in the story of Alcyone and Ceyx (see pages 46-48), as well as with the remarkable story of the Sacred Band of Thebes (see pages 50-51), a military regiment composed entirely of male lovers. In Rome, meanwhile, things get considerably baudier against the backdrop of the dramatic events of Pompeii with the discovery of erotica so eye-widening that it scandalised its nineteenth-century excavators, and was only put on public display in 2000 (see pages 52-57). It seems likely that such scenes would have met with quite the opposite reaction in medieval Europe by those who proudly wore the magnificently profane tin badges that have been found at sites around the continent. The purpose of the

Love A Curious History in 50 Objects

Opposite Top: The Legend of the Baker of Eeklo by Cornelis van Dalem (1530/35-1573/6), a depiction of the popular story about the Belgian town of Eeklo where wives would bring their ugly husbands to the baker to have him magically improve their looks. The baker temporarily placed cabbages on the men's necks while their heads were in the oven.

Opposite Bottom: Husbands bringing their unattractive wives to a windmill, to be transformed into beauties. Engraving by P. Fürst, c.1650.

Right: Lovers Walking in the Snow (Crow and Heron) (1764-72) by Suzuki Harunobu, one of the most romantic of all Japanese ukiyo-e prints. The lovers stroll in the snow intimately sharing an umbrella like they share their love (known as an ai ai gasa pose), perhaps walking a michiyuki, a path to a love suicide, another dramatic device.

badge designs, of what are politely referred to by historians as 'ambulant penises', along with vulvas that climb ladders, sail ships and triumphantly hunt on horseback (see page 58), are a mystery. In this way they sit alongside other puzzles in this book like the Elizabethan portraits of smiling men consumed by flames (see pages 146-147), and Jan van Eyck's masterpiece *Arnolfini Portrait* (see page 100), with its cryptic symbols to decode. See also the gorgeous Unicorn Tapestries (see pages 108-113), which may or may not be some of the most splendid tributes to love ever made, depending on how one interprets their hidden clues.

No book on this subject would be complete without a raft of practical advice to offer, and for those who prefer their love and sex tips to come from some truly experimental and massively unreliable intellectual sources, then you're in luck. Exploring the historical entanglement of love with medicine and magic, for example, leads to the medieval physicians diagnosing love and heartbreak as serious illnesses in need of treatment, as well as the sex quacks who exploited couples desperate to conceive. These include James Graham's pneumatic musical bed of Georgian London, as well as the American con-artist who made millions with his patented and utterly ineffectual procedure of implanting goat testicles in men's scrotums (see pages 178-179).

Indeed, despite these stories having love, marriage and sex as their commonality, they are tales of wildly differing motivations. The story of Dante's work as a tribute of courtly love to Beatrice (see pages 76-78) shares an ambition with the remarkable and previously unpublished illustrated manuscript of Henry Hilditch Bulkeley-Johnson (see pages 212-215). The story of the French noblewoman turned pirate, Jeanne de Clisson, on the other hand, is a tale of furious revenge; while centuries later selfless love would be at the core of the very different naval tale of fellow Frenchwoman Jeanne Baret, the first woman ever to

1852 painting by William Powell Frith (1819-1909), showing the disastrous moment when the poet Alexander Pope (1688-1744) confessed his undying love to Lady Mary Montagu (1689-1762), and she burst out laughing.

circumnavigate the globe, done for the most part disguised in men's clothing (see pages 170-173).

A historical celebration of love should of course be a similarly global journey, and for this book it was important to reach a few of the further flung and overlooked parts (pun *always* intended in this volume), from the legendary sex nuts and birdlike monsters of

the Mauritian islands (see pages 140-145), through the Samarkand mosque, the wedding traditions of the Maya, and the love chains of the Yoruba people of West Africa; until finally we reach the love story that is currently travelling through the vast ocean of interstellar space, and that in all likelihood will still be continuing on its way long after the human race is extinct (see pages 240-243).

The hope for this book is that a browse of its stories and accompanying illustrations will bring with it the same highs, poignancies and occasional horrors of love itself, leaving you as high and bruised as an airborne eighteenth-

century Corsican husband.[1] As a museum of curiosities its exhibits are a collective attempt to record and answer – or rather, a collection of previous attempts to answer – exactly how to define this most mysterious and propulsive force of the human universe. For Joseph Campbell (1904-87), love was 'a friendship set to music'; for Marcel Proust (1871-1922),

Young lovers wander happily into the trap of marriage, in this eighteenth-century engraving.

a 'space and time measured by the heart'. For W. Somerset Maugham, 'love is only a dirty trick played on us to achieve continuation of the species'; while Samuel Johnson took a more pragmatic approach: 'Marriage is the triumph of imagination over intelligence. Second marriage is the triumph of hope over experience.' But perhaps the best philosophy to embrace while diving into these pages is that of the American columnist Franklin P. Jones (1908-80): 'Love doesn't make the world go round,' he wrote. 'Love is what makes the ride worthwhile.'

---

1 In the eighteenth century when a Corsican husband died, his widow's first action was to gather the other local women and toss his corpse up and down on a blanket, in order to see if he was playing dead to escape the marriage. This was reported by Dr Johann August Unzer (1727-99), editor of the medical weekly *Der Arzt. Eine medicinische Wochenschrift*, who claimed the blanket tossing often went on for hours, and that it occasionally 'recalled to life' the man 'who to all appearance had been dead'. His desperate bid for freedom foiled, he was left to the mercy of his former widow.

IL DILETTEVOL GIVOCO

Si gioca con due Dadi douendo ciascuno hauere
auertendo à non fermarsi su i Pellegrini ma cadena
uincera il Gioco, e nel principio facendo 6 e 3 uu à
nell'altre Figure s'osserui il seguente ordine, cive la Sp
si ferma un tiro. Timore si torna indietro sei punti
Gelosia ua alla Rissa e paga un quat: Pericolo ui si sta
q° Liberalità paga un q° e uà all'Occa

Esperienza

Merito

Gelosia

Speranza

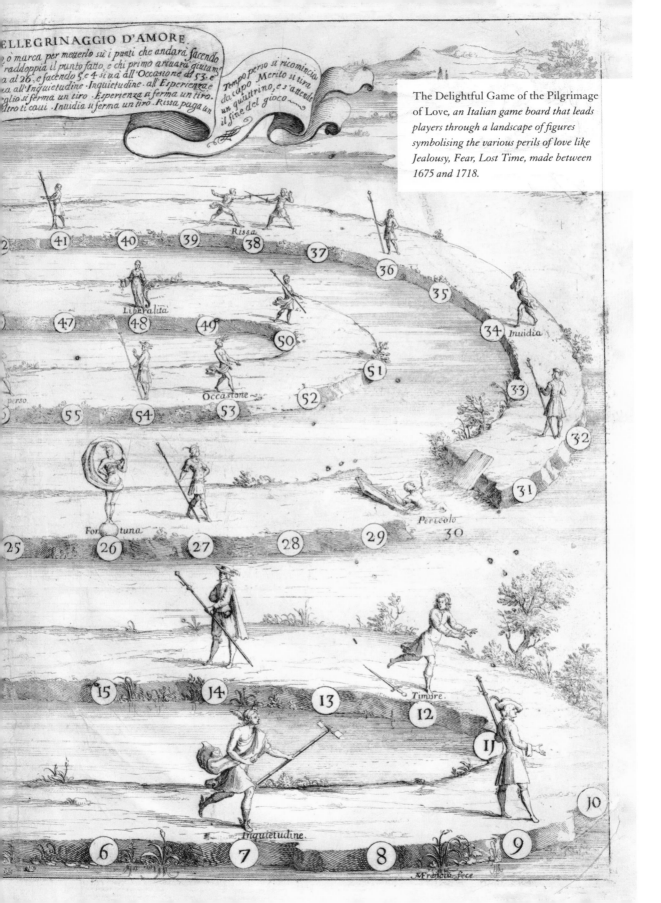

The Delightful Game of the Pilgrimage of Love, *an Italian game board that leads players through a landscape of figures symbolising the various perils of love like Jealousy, Fear, Lost Time, made between 1675 and 1718.*

The Ain Sakhri Lovers (c.9000 BC)

We cannot, of course, know when the oldest kiss took place, but what if we went looking for it? How far back does the path of evidence run before the trail goes cold? This search seemed like the kind of suitably curious challenge with which to begin this book and it eventually led to finding a paper published in 2017 by an anthropologist at Pennsylvania State University named Laura Weyrich, titled *Neanderthal behaviour, diet, and disease inferred from ancient DNA in dental calculus.*

While studying the remains of the last thirteen Neanderthals to walk the Earth, which were found at El Sidrón in northwest Spain, Weyrich was surprised to find that she recognised the genetic signature of a microorganism on one of the teeth – Methanobrevibacter oralis, which is also found in the mouths of modern humans. By comparing the Neanderthal strain with the modern strain, she was able to estimate that the microorganism was transferred between Neanderthals and Homo sapiens roughly 120,000 years ago. This being a period when the two were interbreeding, a likely route for this transfer was kissing. 'When you kiss someone, oral microbes will go back and forth between your mouths,' Weyrich says. 'It could have happened once and then propagated … But it could also be something that occurred more regularly.'

As we move on hastily from this imagery, for the earliest documentary evidence of human intimacy in a more solid state – specifically, carved into calcite cobble – we find the prehistoric figurine known as the Ain Sakhri Lovers. Created by a member of the Natufian culture approximately 11,000 years ago in 9000 BC, the 102mm-high sculpture shows a faceless couple of indeterminate gender engaged in a sexual embrace, the earliest such depiction known. Despite its age of many millennia, it was only discovered in 1933, when a French consul in Jerusalem named René Neuville recognised its importance among the recent finds made by Bedouin at Ain Sakhri caves near Bethlehem.

In contrast to other recovered Natufian artworks made of antler and bone, the *Lovers* is a remarkably clever sculpture. Its artist incorporates the natural heart – and phallic shape – of the stone, along with the chattermarks that show it once bounced along the bed of a stream or river, to form the two figures embracing each other face-to-face. The work was painstaking. The possibly love-struck sculptor would have used a stone chisel or antler hammer to pick out the couple from the calcite surface. 'It is the oldest known sculpture of people making love and has a timeless, touching resonance of tenderness, love and relationship,' read its British Museum curator notes. 'It has always been popular with museum visitors and acquired a new modern symbolism during the period of lockdown against Coronavirus in 2020, when it epitomised the simple but essential need for the reassurance of a hug that had to be avoided at that time.'

Left: Over 24,000 years before the sculptor of the Ain Sakhri Lovers was carving his work, another prehistoric artist in the Hohle Fels (German for 'hollow rock') cave in the Swabian Jura of south-western Germany picked up a tusk of a woolly mammoth and carved the earliest known depiction of a human being. The oldest of the Palaeolithic Venus figures discovered around Europe, the Venus of Hohle Fels bears exaggerated buttocks, genitals and breasts, while her legs and arms are stumpy, suggesting that it is her sexual features that are the focus. The meaning of these figures has long been the subject of debate, but they are commonly thought to be fertility symbols, perhaps even of fertility deities, of enough significance to justify the immensely time-consuming process of carving them using primitive tools.

Right: A distinctly phallic object carved around 30,000 years ago, one example of objects carefully referred to in the scholarship as 'Ice-Age batons', found in the Hohle Fels cave. 'Looking at the size, shape, and – in some cases – explicit symbolism of the Ice Age batons, it seems disingenuous to avoid the most obvious and straightforward interpretation,' says the British archaeologist Timothy Taylor, 'but it has been avoided.' The batons might have been multi-purpose, as there is evidence from wear that this example was also used as a hammer.

Opposite: Fast-forward to twelfth-century Europe and we find the Sheela na gig grotesque carvings on churches such as this at the Church of St Mary and St David, built c.1140 at Kilpeck, Herefordshire, England. One theory as to their origin and reason behind their exaggerated vulva is that they represent a pagan fertility goddess; another is that they were used to ward off death, evil and misfortune.

The Seated Woman of Çatalhöyük (c.6000 BC), and Other Ancient Gods of Love and Lust

It might seem strange that, of all the infamous deities crowding the pantheon of love gods throughout history, the lesser-known figure shown to the left should be chosen to open this chapter. But this baked-clay statue of a nude woman seated between two animal-headed armrests is an extraordinary artefact. Known as the Seated Woman of Çatalhöyük, it was created c.6000 BC by a Neolithic artist and discovered nearly 8,000 years later in its eponymous Turkish region in 1961. While there are clear similarities with the exaggerated figures of the Venus fertility deities mentioned on page 21, this is also one of the earliest known examples of the 'mistress of animals', a thrillingly mysterious motif that runs through ancient art of the Near East and Egypt.

The powerful image of a female deity accompanied by wild animals either side of her is thought to have fed into the development of numerous female gods in other later cultures, including the elaborate storied mythology of the ancient Greeks. In this small clay figure, then, it's possible that what we are looking at is an embryonic form of Aphrodite.

Associated with love, lust, beauty, pleasure, passion and copulation, Aphrodite was married to Hephaistos, god of blacksmiths, who forged for the gods weapons and stranger devices like autonomous tripods that walked themselves to Mount Olympus. The marriage was not a suitable match and Aphrodite enjoyed a steady parade of lovers, including Ares, god of war. On Earth, a festival called the Aphrodisiac was held regularly in her honour at her temple in Corinth, where worshippers paid her homage by having rollicking sex sessions with her priestesses.[1]

While Aphrodite (Venus to the Romans) is perhaps the best-known love god today, it's worth casting around for comparable figures in other ancient belief systems to get a sense of how the power of romantic love was accounted for, and to whom appeals were made for help with its affairs. For the ancient Egyptians it was Hathor, wife of the sun god Ra. Worship of Hathor originated in the third millennium BC, when she begins to appear most commonly in the form of a cow, as a symbol of her maternal association. More Egyptian temples are dedicated to her than any other deity. Those desperate to conceive sent her their prayers, and through to the first millennium BC women hoped to be assimilated with her in the next world. One detail we learn about Hathor from a story found in the tomb of King Tutankhamen is that she can't handle her drink. In *The Destruction of Mankind* narrative, Ra bids her to become the war goddess Sekhmet to punish humans for their sins. Hathor gets a little carried away, however, and just as she's poised to obliterate every

The statue of the Aphrodite of Syracuse, dated to the second century AD.

---

1 Incidentally, worship of Aphrodite was active in the twentieth century, not in Greece but Long Island, New York. The Church of Aphrodite was founded in 1939 by Gleb Botkin (1900-69), a Russian émigré and son of Dr Yevgeny Botkin, the Russian court physician who was murdered at Yekaterinburg by the Bolsheviks with Tsar Nicholas II and his family on 17 July 1918. Botkin believed that it was the patriarchy that was to blame for all the issues plaguing mankind. 'Men!' he once cried. 'Just look at the mess we've made!'

The Queen of the Night relief, featuring the love goddess Inanna/Ishtar.

across millennia; as early as 4000 BC she was venerated in Sumer, becoming the most widely worshipped deity with temples across Mesopotamia. (It turns out that a love goddess cult whose primary activities are the practising of sex rituals holds quite a broad appeal.) The later Akkadians and Babylonians absorbed Sumerian culture and deities into their pantheon, as did the Assyrians, who adored Inanna/Ishtar and promoted her to the head of their pantheon. One finds allusions to her in the Hebrew Bible, and she is said to have influenced the Ugaritic Ashtart and later Phoenician Astarte deities, who in turn influenced the myth-building of the Greek Aphrodite. Inanna/Ishtar enjoyed a thriving following until her popularity began to decline between the first and sixth centuries AD, with the rise of Christianity. You can find her in the British Museum, however, as the winged subject of one of the most famous objects in the collection – the baked clay panel known as the Queen of the Night relief (shown here), dated to the nineteenth-eighteenth century BC.

person on Earth, Ra manages to get her drunk. A sloshed Hathor forgets her murderous designs, resumes her love-goddessing, and things return to normal. (Although another story tells of how she later dances a striptease to cheer up her father, so 'normal' might not be quite the right word.)

For the ancient Sumerians, their goddess of love, war and fertility was Inanna, later known as Ishtar to the Akkadians, Babylonians and Assyrians. All gods are immortal, yet all die through the extinction, or shift in belief, of their faithful. Inanna is quite remarkable in that her lifespan encompassed different cultures

Love Gods Around the World

Manmatha, also known as Kama or Kamadeva, Hindu god of love. He is usually represented as a young man, mounted on a parrot, with a bow in his hand. The wood of the bow is a sugar cane; the cord is sometimes composed of a string of bees, and his five arrows match the number of senses that love overrides.

Left: The Aztec goddess of love (on the right), Xochiquetzal ('precious feather flower' in the Nahuatl language). Because of her great beauty she suffered at the hands of the misogynistic gods – while still married to the rain god Tlaloc, she was kidnapped by the god of the night Tezcatlipoca and forced to marry him, thereby gaining her throne as the goddess of love. By another husband she also gave birth to Quetzalcoatl, the feathered serpent god.

Above Left: Tu Er Shen (literally 'rabbit deity', as he was known when he was mortal) is a lesser-known deity of Chinese mythology – the god of male homosexual love and marriage. Born in the Qing dynasty, Hu Tianbao fell in love with a local government official and spied on him while he was bathing. He was discovered and beaten to death. The gods of the underworld took pity on him and revived him as the god of homosexual relationships.

Above: Oshun, or Ọṣun, is the goddess of beauty and erotic love in the Yoruba-based religions of West Africa. Associated with freshwater and purity, she is the patron saint of the Osun River in Nigeria, which bears her name, and is often depicted as a mermaid.

Left: This fourteenth-century Japanese Buddhist hanging scroll shows Aizen Myōō, blood-red Wisdom King of Passion, who symbolises how the violent energies of carnality and desire can be channelled into the pursuit of enlightenment. Aizen Myōō is a figure of rage: his hair on end, a snarling lion rising from his head, his six arms wielding weapons. Despite (or perhaps because of) his fearsome appearance, it was he whom the love-afflicted called on for help.

This large appliqué of nineteenth-century Tibet
shows the Vajrayana goddess Kurukulla, beautiful
bewitcher of men. Reciting her mantra is believed to
grant the power of subduing any man, including
kings. The four-armed figure's red skin corresponds
to her status as an emanation of the red Amitabha
Buddha. Just like Manmatha/Kamadeva, she fires
flower-tipped arrows, but is considerably more
ferocious, as we can tell from subtle clues like her
headdress of skulls, bone ornaments, and the fact that
she's dancing on a pile of corpses.

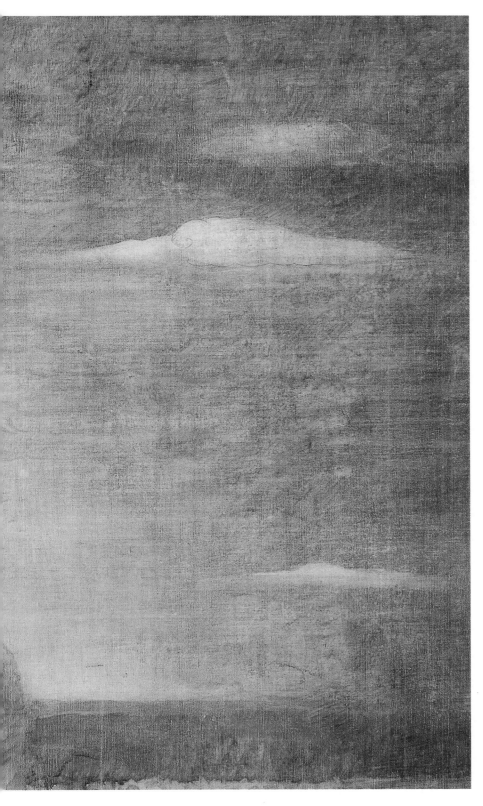

In Norse mythology
Freyja, or Frigga, was the
wife of Odin and goddess
of fertility and marriage.
As Queen of Fólkvangr,
a hall similar to Valhalla,
she took care of those
who died in battle, but
spent a lot of her time
searching the Earth for
her wandering husband,
crying tears of red gold
as she rode her chariot
pulled by cats.

The Marriage of Inanna and Dumuzid
– *Love in Ancient Mesopotamia*

Among the more than 30,000 clay tablets and fragments recovered from the great library at Nineveh of Ashurbanipal, king of the Neo-Assyrian Empire from 669 to 631 BC, is a text that describes a particularly injurious illness. 'When the patient is continually clearing his throat; is often lost for words; is always talking to himself when he is quite alone and laughing for no reason in the corners of fields; is habitually depressed; his throat tight; finds no pleasure in eating or drinking; endlessly repeating, with great sighs, "Ah, my poor heart!" – he is suffering from lovesickness. For a man and for a woman, it is all one and the same.'

For the Ancient Mesopotamians, love held the same profundity as it does in modern civilisations. We can recognise this in the titles of their 'love songs', with their lyrics that share the sentiments of those composed by lovestruck teenage bedroom musicians today – 'Sleep, begone! I want to hold my darling in my arms!'; 'When you speak to me, you make my heart swell till I could die!'; and 'I did not close my eyes last night; Yes, I was awake all night long, my darling [thinking of you]'; to name but a few of the hits.[1]

At the same time, marriage was approached with the same businesslike pragmatism as any other financial affair. For the Sumerians, the word for 'love' was a transactional verb that literally meant 'to measure the earth', i.e. 'to mark off land'. For them, as well as for the Babylonians and Assyrians, marriage was fundamentally a monetary arrangement that cemented an orderly society and ensured procreation. Families usually organised the pairing, but there were other matchmaking methods available. For the ancient Babylonian searching for a wife, for example, should family connections not be helpful then

according to Herodotus in his *Histories* (1:196) another option was bidding at public bridal auctions:

Once a year in each village the young women eligible to marry were collected all together in one place while the men stood around them in a circle. Then a herald called up the young women one by one and offered them for sale. He began with the most beautiful. When she was sold for a high price, he offered for sale the one who ranked next in beauty. All of them were then sold to be wives. The richest of the Babylonians who wished to wed bid against each other for the loveliest young women, while the commoners, who were not concerned about beauty, received the uglier women along with monetary compensation …

Even when the marital arrangement was made, the practical details of the union were often worked out ahead of the nuptials with marriage contracts. The oldest surviving marriage contract in history is an agreement made around 4,000 years ago between an Assyrian couple, named Laqipum and his bride, Hatala. The main stipulation is a contingency plan in the event that Hatala

---

1 As collected by the historian Jean Bottéro in *Everyday Life in Ancient Mesopotamia* (1992).

Opposite: An ancient Sumerian depiction of the marriage of Inanna and Dumuzid.

The oldest surviving marriage contract.

is unable to produce a child within the first two years of marriage. Should this happen, she agrees to buy a slave woman known as a *hierodule* to sleep with her husband and act as a surrogate. When the child is born, the *hierodule* would be given her freedom. The cuneiform tablet was only discovered in 2017, at Kültepe, a district within the central Turkish province of Kayseri, and as well as being the oldest prenuptial agreement, is also the earliest known mention of infertility.

If we venture beyond legal literature, in all of the surviving storytelling of the ancient Sumerians, the most commonly told love story is that of the previously mentioned deity Inanna, goddess of love, sex and war; and her husband Dumuzid, god of shepherds and provider of milk. The poem 'Inanna Prefers the Farmer', for example, tells the story of

their early courtship, when Inanna initially chooses a farmer over Dumuzid the shepherd, until he demonstrates that his gifts would always better those of his rival. But we learn a lot more of their relationship from the fantastic amount of erotic poetry written of the couple's consummation of marriage. 'A Balbale to Inanna' is one such work, translated by the Assyriologists Diane Wolkstein and Samuel Noah Kramer, with a typical verse reading:

My vulva, the horn,
The Boat of Heaven,
Is full of eagerness like the young moon.
My untilled land lies fallow.
As for me, Inanna,
Who will plow my vulva?

Who will plow my high field?
Who will plow my wet ground?

In the great Sumerian tale *Descent of Inanna into the Underworld*, Inanna leaves her husband to travel to Kur, the underworld, to visit her sister the goddess Ereshkigal, who rules from the giant underground palace Ganzir. Inanna travels to the walls of the underworld city, demanding entry through its series of seven gates. Ereshkigal agrees, but orders that each gate through which she must pass be opened by just a crack, forcing Inanna to squeeze through by removing a piece of clothing at each gate, which gradually strips her literally, and symbolically, of her power. By the time Inanna reaches Ereshkigal's court she is naked, but still manages to take Ereshkigal's place. The group of deities in residence known as the Anunnaki are outraged by this and turn Inanna into a corpse hanging by a hook.

Ereshkigal eventually consents to her sister's corpse being sprinkled with the food and water of life to be revived, but there's a catch: Ereshkigal's *galla* (demons) demand that one of the living must take her place. They magically show her several figures going about their life on the surface, from whom she must choose a replacement. Not

The Babylonian Marriage Market *(1875) by Edwin Longsden Long.*

her servant Ninshubur, Inanna says, for he is loyal; not Shara, her beautician, for he is seen mourning her death. The demons then suggest her husband, Dumuzid, who is revealed to be dealing with his grief rather admirably, spending his days sitting on his wife's throne in lavish clothing and cavorting with slave girls. An irate Inanna immediately instructs the demons to take him, and Dumuzid is dragged down to the netherworld, lipstick marks still fresh on his collar, while Inanna retakes her place in the upper world with not even a backwards glance.

Above: An Old Babylonian plaque dating to the first half of the second millennium BC, of a male and a female engaged in sexual intercourse, discovered in southern Iraq.

Opposite: An erotic terracotta carving dating to the Old Babylonian Period (c.1830 BC–c.1531 BC). One popular interpretation of these plaques is that they depict a sacred marriage ritual performed annually during the Sumerian new year festival, in which the king assumes the role of Dumuzid and engages in sexual intercourse with the court's high priestess of Inanna, performing the role of the goddess.

Yuny and His Wife Renenutet (c.1294-1279 BC)—Love in Ancient Egypt

With the affection of this married couple emanating so vibrantly and relatably, it is extraordinary to think that this statue was carved over 3,300 years ago. It shows the chief royal scribe (and possibly also physician) Yuny, of the city of Asyut, sitting beside his wife Renenutet, who has her arm wrapped lovingly around her husband. The inscriptions at the base elaborate on Yuny's official roles and responsibilities, while the symbols in the centre pleat of his skirt read, 'May everything that comes forth upon the offering table of [the god] … and all pure food that comes forth from the Great Enclosure [the temple complex at Heliopolis] be for the chief scribe, royal scribe of letters, Yuny, justified.' Renenutet, meanwhile, holds in her left hand a *menat* necklace, which was ceremoniously shaken like cymbals when entering the presence of the goddess Hathor and other deities. Traces of black pigment remain on the wigs (the couple were once fully painted in glorious colour).

On the reverse of the statue we find still more details of the ancient Egyptian ideals of love and affection. Two relief scenes show the couple receiving offerings from their dutiful son, while below Renenutet respectfully offers food and drink to her own parents.

There was no tradition of grand wedding ceremonies in ancient Egypt. The union was arranged by the parents, an exchange of goods and the price of the bride agreed upon, and the deal was sealed when the bride moved into the groom's house with her belongings. Marriage was an arrangement viewed practically as stabilizing the community, one that could

The relief scenes on the reverse of the statue.

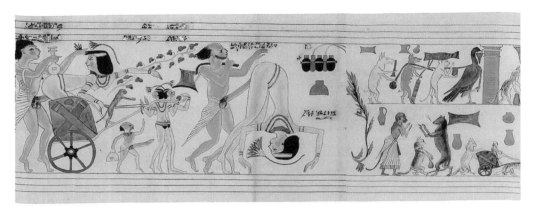

be used for personal advancement, but there is also evidence of the more romantic notions of modern sensibilities. Papyri carry rapturous tributes to wives, like the lyrical waxing of the besotted author of the Chester Beatty Papyrus I of *c*.1200 BC: 'No one can rival her, for she is the most beautiful woman alive. Look, she is like Sirius, which marks the beginning of a good year. She radiates perfection and glows with health. The glance of her eye is gorgeous. Her lips speak sweetly, and not one word too many. Long-necked and milky breasted she is, her hair the colour of pure lapis. Gold is nothing compared to her arms and her fingers are like lotus flowers. Her buttocks are full, but her waist is narrow. As for her thighs – they only add to her beauty.'

There is also the more mournful, a coffin inscription from the 21st Dynasty that records a husband lamenting the death of his wife: 'Woe,

A modern reconstruction of a segment of the Turin Erotic Papyrus, created c.1150 BC. *The first third of the papyrus shows animals performing human tasks, while the remaining two segments bear vignettes of men and women in various sex positions. When the French orientalist Jean-François Champollion saw the papyrus in 1824, he described it as 'an image of monstrous obscenity that gave me a really strange impression about Egyptian wisdom and composure'.*

you have been taken from me, the one with the beautiful face; there was none like her and I found nothing bad about you.' The inscription is signed 'your brother and mate' (husbands were often called 'brothers', and wives 'sisters'), and indeed numerous other similar inscriptions support the idea that to Egyptians of this period, men and women were viewed as equal partners and friends in a relationship, and that while the man was the head of the household, women were not subservient to him.

Almost no information survives on sexual practices in ancient Egypt, save for scant erotic details in illustrations, and there is also very little evidence for prostitution. There was no word for 'virgin', and no prohibitions on homosexuality; in fact several fragments of papyrus allude to Pepi II (*c*.2278-2184 BC) engaging in a homosexual relationship with a military commander, although this is disputed. Single women were free to sleep with whomever they chose, but precautions were taken. The Ebers Medical Papyrus, written *c*.1542 BC, offers recipes for contraceptives, including: 'Prescription to make a woman cease to become pregnant for one, two or three years: Grind together finely a measure of acacia dates with some honey. Moisten seed-wool with the mixture and insert.'

Married life was sweet, but short – not because divorce was rife (although the option

The tomb of Khnumhotep and Niânkhnum, here depicted in an embrace, was discovered in 1964 in the necropolis of Saqqara, in the region of Memphis, in Egypt. The two men shared the role of 'confidants of the king' in the palace of Pharaoh Niouserra, the sixth ruler of the Fifth Dynasty, around 2460-2430 BC. Their bodies were found entwined, with their faces nose-to-nose (a traditional position for spouses), while the sepulchre they share bears the epitaph: 'Khnumhotep and Niankhkhnum lived together and loved each other with passion.' At first it was interpreted the two were brothers, but it's now believed they were a same-sex couple.

was available and not taboo), but because lifespans were short. Men on average lived to their thirties, while women often died in childbirth as young as sixteen. But Egyptian marriage was not just for the earthly plain; the union continued into the afterlife, as did one's sex life – Egyptian mummies have been discovered with false penises attached, in preparation for the activity, while mummified female corpses have been found with artificial nipples.[1] Both would become functional in the next life, which was not the dazzling golden-gated paradise of Christianity but simply a continuation of one's life before death, with one's spouse, one's belongings, and even favourite pets, in the Fields of Reeds. Which is why it was so important to treat your spouse well in life, in case they died and took their revenge from beyond the grave by preventing you from joining them in the Fields. In this unfortunate event there was, luckily, recourse one could take: a priest could provide you with a spell to break this curse – for a modest fee, of course.

Opposite: A statue of a family that served as a domestic icon, c.1353-1336 BC, New Kingdom, Amarna Period. Each member of the group is male – thought to be a family of a grandfather, a father and a son.

Below: An erotic scene from a fragment of a leather hanging, c.1550-1458 BC, found in debris in a Middle Kingdom tomb two hundred yards east of Hatshepsut's temple at Deir el-Bahri.

---

[1] One under-reported fact about Tutankhamen is that he was embalmed in an equally unusual way, with his penis mummified erect at a 90-degree angle – the only known mummy to possess such a feature. One theory as to why he was buried this way is that it was an attempt to turn him into the form of Osiris, the god of the underworld, as literally as possible. The erect penis references Osiris's regenerative powers and is similar to the design of 'corn-mummies', which are non-human artificial mummies created in later periods in honour of Osiris. Alas, Tutankhamen's godly stiffy was snapped off shortly after the discovery of his tomb.

The Fuxi and Nüwa Scroll (eighth century) – Love Stories of Ancient China

In the same way that someone today might carry a can of pepper spray for self-defence, the ladies of the imperial courts of ancient China's Forbidden City were armed against unwanted male attention with a deterrent that had a bit more bite. The story goes that miniature Pekingese 'sleeve dogs' were so called because that's exactly where you would find them, secreted in the sleeves of courtiers, ready to be deployed like furry little missiles to scare away threats. The breed standards of the time even discuss the requirement of specific colours of the dog's coat to stealthily blend in with the outfits of its owner – golden sable variants of the 'lion dogs' go splendidly with yellow robes, for example.

Curiously, sleeves are a link to a famous love affair in ancient Chinese history known as 'The Cut Sleeve'. Emperor Ai of Han (27 BC-1 BC) of the Chinese Han dynasty was twenty years old when he rose to the throne in succession to his childless uncle, Emperor Cheng (51 BC-7 BC). His was a relatively short reign, from 7 BC to 1 BC, but in such little amount of time was involved in an impressive amount of corruption and the levying of crippling taxes on the people. He is best remembered, though, for his homosexual relationship (they were tolerated at the time, as long as they didn't interfere with one's heterosexual marriage) with an official in his imperial administration named Dong Xian, who enjoyed a speedy rise to power thanks to his intimacy with the emperor. The idiomatic term for homosexuality in Chinese, *duanxiu zhi pi* (literally 'passion of the cut sleeve') originates in a story of this relationship, in which the two men fell asleep together on the same straw mat. Rather than tug his sleeve out from under the head of his sleeping lover, Emperor Ai cut off the sleeve instead.

Another slang phrase for same-sex love in China is 'the bitten peach', which dates back to Duke Ling of Wey, twenty-eighth ruler (from

*c.*534 BC to 492 BC) of the ancient Chinese state of Wey, who is the subject of Chapter 15 in the *Analects* of Confucius. The story goes that Duke Ling favoured a courtier named Mizi Xia, whom he permitted to use the ducal carriage, and who captured his admiration by sharing with the duke the remainder of an especially delicious and plump peach. The story becomes a parable, however, when Mizi Xia's looks fade: the duke loses interest in his lover, accuses him of having stolen the carriage and of insulting the duke by giving him a half-eaten peach. The bitten peach is a symbol still used to signify love between men in China today.

There are many love-related sayings in modern Chinese language, even if the concept of romantic love is not as historically prevalent as in other cultures (there is no word for 'romance', for example). 'Having love, drinking water will fill you up, without love, eating food will leave you hungry', is one, while 'Love the house with its crows (on the roof)' is a useful way of saying 'take the bad with the good'. Then there's 'In the eyes of a lover, Xi Shi appears', a curious expression roughly similar to 'beauty is in the eye of the beholder'. It refers to one of a group of four infamous female figures of Chinese love

An eighth-century hanging scroll of Fuxi and Nüwa, twin brother and sister of Chinese creation mythology. Fuxi and Nüwa were the two original living creatures on Earth, who inhabited the mythical Kunlun Mountain. One day they decided to become husband and wife, and created offspring from clay, which they brought alive with divine magic – these were the first humans.

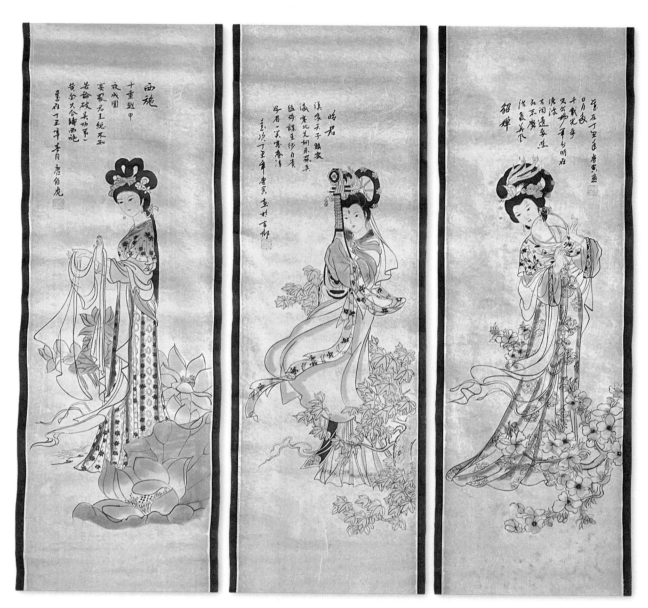

西施
十重越甲
夜戎圍
宴罷兒王絕不知
若論破吳功第一
黃金久合鑄西施
壽石丁丑年青唐伯虎

昭君
漢家天子鎮衣
滅盡北兵柳未落
臨母謙至紗白賣
妤君一笑對春清
丁丑年書寫 畫於古都

貂蟬
壽在丁丑年唐伯虎
千載光年
又名鄉年分明在
淡淡左閒逢家逢
孔不慶
沿氣美盡

legend known as the 'Four Beauties', who each
in their time caught the eye of an emperor
or ruler and subsequently greatly impacted
Chinese history.

Historical evidence of Xi Shi, Wang
Zhaojun, Diaochan and Yang Guifei is scant,
but the four women who are thought of as
the most beautiful in all of Chinese history
are wrapped in millennia of legend, and
continue to exist today in the aforementioned

*Above and Opposite Left: The Four Beauties
of ancient Chinese history, infamous for their
sway over besotted emperors and kings.*

phrase, and other widely used complimentary
proverbs. These include 'Xi Shi sinks fish',
which refers to Xi Shi (seventh century-sixth
century BC) possessing so great a beauty that
she caused fish to forget how to swim and
they sank. 'Wang Zhaojun entices birds into

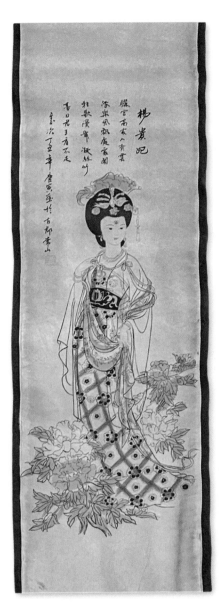

'愛', the traditional Chinese Mandarin character for romantic love, which has its centre the character for heart, '心'. Older Mandarin speakers find the use of the character in this way a little too 肉麻 (ròumá, 'corny', or 'cheesy'), and instead use 喜歡／喜欢 (xǐhuan, 'to like') instead.

falling' refers to a woman born around 50 BC and a member of the harem of Emperor Yun. She was never visited by Yun, however, as he was put off by her portrait, a deliberately unflattering likeness painted by a vindictive artist whom Wang Zhaojun had refused to bribe. When the emperor eventually discovered her beauty, he immediately had the artist executed. 'Diaochan eclipses the Moon' originates with the claim that Diaochan

(c. AD 220-280) had looks so luminous that she caused the Moon to hide itself in shame.

'Yang Guifei shames flowers' is more tragic. In the eighth century Emperor Xuanzong of Tang was deeply in love with the beautiful Yang Guifei, but when he and his cortège were forced to flee during the An Lushan Rebellion, his guards blamed the uprising on the consort and her family and demanded he have her executed. The emperor reluctantly had her strangled, enshrining her as the most tragic figure in Chinese romantic writing. Today, all four history-loaded proverbs are often combined into one phrase by lovers paying tribute to the beauty of their intended.

Dead Man's Fingers –
Ceyx and Alcyone

Marriage for the ancient Greeks was approached with practical and social benefit in mind and procreation as the main purpose, and so it is little wonder that we find in their mythology wondrous tales of passionate romances. Especially interesting are the stories of which traces have survived to modern culture; for example, the phrase 'halcyon days', used to describe an ideal time period. This originates from the Greek myth of Ceyx, king of the city-state of Trachis, and his wife Alcyone, daughter of King Aeolus of Aeolia. According to the *Bibliotheca* of Pseudo-Apollodorus, a compendium of myths written sometime in the first or second century, the blissfully happy couple initiated their tragedy by playfully referring to each other as 'Zeus' and 'Hera'. Though not intended to be sacrilegious, this angered Zeus, who, as other myths show, needed little excuse to exercise an itchy trigger finger.

When Ceyx left on a sea voyage (as Ovid tells us, to consult an oracle about his predicament), leaving his queen behind out of fears for her safety, Zeus hurled a lightning bolt at Ceyx's ship, which caused it to capsize. As Ceyx drowned, he begged the gods with his last breath that his body be returned to his wife. Alcyone, meanwhile, was visited by Morpheus, the god of dreams, who appeared in the form of her husband to tell her of his demise. Distraught, Alcyone threw herself into the sea to join Ceyx in death. Out of pity, the gods

Right: A fresco discovered at Pompeii of the myth of Leda and the swan, in which Zeus morphs into the bird and forces himself on Leda. As a result, she bears Helen and Polydeuces, children of Zeus, in two eggs, while also simultaneously bearing Castor and Clytemnestra, children of her husband Tyndareus, the King of Sparta.

Opposite: Charles-André van Loo, Ceyx and Alcyone, 1750.

Above: Alcyonium digitatum, *also known as Dead Man's Fingers.*

Opposite: Pygmalion and Galatea (c.1890), by Jean-Léon Gérôme (1824-1904). In Greek mythology Pygmalion was a legendary king of Cyprus. He takes up celibacy after witnessing the lascivious shenanigans of the Propoetides of the city of Amathus, who according to Ovid's Metamorphoses *were 'the first to prostitute their bodies and their reputations in public, and, losing all sense of shame, they lost the power to blush, as the blood hardened in their cheeks, and only a small change turned them into hard flints'. To distract himself Pygmalion took up sculpture and carved a woman out of ivory who was so perfect that he named her Galatea and fell in love with her. At the altar of Aphrodite Pygmalion wished that he would meet someone as beautiful as his statue. When he returned home, he kissed Galatea's lips and found they were soft and warm. Aphrodite had granted his wish and brought the statue to life.*

transformed the couple into seaborne birds called Halcyons, that we today know as kingfishers. The belief at the time was that the kingfisher laid its eggs in a nest on the shore; the sample of soft coral shown here is *Alcyonium digitatum* (also known as Dead Man's Fingers, for obvious reasons), which was named after Pliny's belief that it was the marine nest of the Halcyon bird. The gods ordered that during the nesting period at the height of winter, the seas be calm and the weather still, so as not to interfere. These were the halcyon days.

The Lion of Chaeronea (c.338 BC) – The Story of the Sacred Band of Thebes

On 3 June 1818 the British architect George Ledwell Taylor (1788-1883) was crossing a field near the village of Chaeronea while using Pausanias's *Description of Greece* as a tourist guide, when he tripped over what turned out to be a piece of marble jutting from the ground. The stone appeared to be sculpted, and with the help of local farmers he and his friends uncovered the enormous head of a stone lion, as shown opposite. Astonishingly this appeared to be the same lion that Pausanias mentions being erected as a monument to mark the burial of an extraordinary legion of men.

When the site was eventually excavated in the late nineteenth century a mass burial was indeed discovered: the skeletons of 254 men, arranged in seven rows, found within an enclosure by the monument. This fighting unit was known as the Sacred Band of Thebes, remarkable for their ferocity, martial skill and for the fact that they were composed entirely of pairs of male lovers, who fought side-by-side for freedom of Thebes from the hegemony of Sparta in the fourth century BC.

Most Greek armies were comprised of part-time fighters, citizen-soldiers who took up arms when called upon. The Sacred Band was the first professional state-funded standing army in Greek history, with its unique hiring policy based on the idea that men completely devoted and loyal to each other would form an unstoppable cohesive unit. This emotional bond between the soldiers was the 'sacred' nature of the band, a sacrosanctity that, according to both Plutarch and Aristotle, same-sex male lovers of Thebes would confirm with each other at the shrine of Iolaus, nephew and lover of Hercules.

While a military corps of male lovers was unique, in ancient Greek life homosexual relationships were so common as to be a kind of rite of passage, and usually took the form of an athletic male in his late teens (the *eromenos*, or 'the beloved') partnering with an older man (the *erastes*, or 'the lover') in a relationship that was often but not necessarily sexual, and also pedagogical – the older man would mentor the youth in philosophy, politics and poetry. The ancient Greeks had no equivalent of the modern sense of sexual orientation in terms of 'straight' or 'gay'; the same men would be expected to go on in later life to marry women and to raise families. But while this was an attitude to be found across Greece, the Thebans were the first to weaponise it.

The earliest known record of the Sacred Band referred to by name was made in 324 BC, in the oration *Against Demosthenes* by the Athenian writer Dinarchus, who tells of the Sacred Band being led by the general Pelopidas. Fighting alongside the units commanded by Epaminondas, who led the army of Thebes (Boeotia), the Band were part of the force that significantly defeated the Spartans at the Battle of Leuctra in 371 BC. Plutarch (AD 46-120), who originated from the village of Chaeronea where the lion was found, is the main source of the Band's exploits, writing that they were put together by the boeotarch Gorgidas, following the routing of the Spartan force occupying the Theban citadel of Cadmea.

The Lion of Chaeronea, marking the mass grave of the Sacred Band of Thebes, in a photograph taken in 1907.

The most famous reference to the Band, however, is made in Plato's *Symposium* (*c.*380 BC), during a speech by the character Phaedrus in which he refers to an 'army of lovers'. A group of Athenian aristocrats enjoying a banquet begin musing on the topic of love. One of the guests, Phaedrus, lyricises on the loyalty that love brings, and wonders about its use in the martial arena:

If by some contrivance a city, or an army, of lovers and their young loves could come into being … then, fighting alongside one another, such men, though few in number, could defeat practically all humankind. For a man in love would rather have anyone other than his lover see him leave his place in the line or toss away his weapons, and often would rather die on behalf of the one he loves.

According to Plutarch, the Sacred Band troops were initially dispersed among the front ranks of regular infantry, but in 375 BC the younger boeotarch Pelopidas took command and forged them into a single unit of shock troops whose principal task was to charge straight for, and kill, the enemy's best fighters and leaders. They quickly gained a formidable reputation and regularly dispatched forces that often greatly outnumbered their own, puncturing the myth of Spartan invincibility.

Their eventual defeat came at the Battle of Chaeronea (338 BC), when the Theban army and its allies were scattered by the novel long spears of the Macedonian forces of Philip II and his son Alexander. Surrounded, the Sacred Band stood fast, fighting for each other, until they were eventually overwhelmed. Plutarch writes that upon seeing their corpses piled high and learning of their identity, Philip II wept and declared, 'Perish any man who suspects that these men either did or suffered anything unseemly.'

Love in Ancient Rome – From Pompeii's Erotica, to Hadrian and Antinous (c.123)

When Mount Vesuvius violently erupted in the autumn of AD 79, it projected a massive, lethal cloud of super-heated tephra and gases 33 km (21 miles) into the sky, along with molten rock, pumice and hot ash at a rate of 1.5 million tons per second. The thermal energy released was ultimately 100,000 times that of the atomic bombs on Hiroshima and Nagasaki. Caught in the pyroclastic surges, and submerged under the ashfalls, were the towns of Herculaneum and Pompeii and their combined estimated populations of 20,000 people. Excavations of these sites, frozen in time, began in the eighteenth century. By the early 1800s, temperatures were – so to speak – beginning to rise again, due to the unexpectedly large volume of one kind of discovery: erotic art. The archaeologists of that stiffly reserved era were confronted with an absolute embarrassment of phalluses and graphic sexual depictions everywhere they looked, in frescoes and statues, and in the design of everyday objects like the bronze brazier supported by a tripod of ithyphallic satyrs, shown opposite, recovered from the House of Julia Felix in Pompeii.

While it was Spanish excavators under the orders of Charles III of Spain who began the looting of Pompeii's ash-covered treasures in the late eighteenth century, it was the French in 1806 who set about digging up the site in its entirety, a dig that continued even when control of Naples reverted to the Spanish under Ferdinand I. Frescoes, furniture, statues and jewellery were removed en masse and moved to the Museo Archeologico Nazionale di Napoli. A French guide (with illustrations, of course) of the erotic Pompeian treasures was published in 1816, becoming desperately sought-after; but in 1819, Ferdinand's son Francis I visited the museum with his wife and young family and was scandalised by the explicit art. Every item of a sexual nature was ordered locked in a *Gabinetto Segreto* (secret cabinet), where only scholars with special permission, or those who paid the best bribes, could gain access. In the Pompeian ruins, metal shutters were placed over the erotica, opened to male tourists willing to pay a fee. The *Gabinetto Segreto* was bricked up in 1849 and only opened to the public in 2000.

Perhaps one factor in the notoriously laid-back Roman attitudes to sex was their reliance on the contraceptive properties of a miracle plant they called 'silphium', which was of such rarity, and of which they devoured such quantities, that it was driven to extinction. Today there is no consensus as to the identity of this plant with which antiquity was so obsessed, but it's thought likely to have been in the *Ferula* genus (giant fennel), or perhaps *Thapsia*, a poisonous genus otherwise known

Opposite: 'Pan copulating with goat' – one of the most famous objects in the Naples Museum collection, recovered from Pompeii.

Bronze brazier and its excited satyrs, recovered from the House of Julia Felix in Pompeii.

as 'deadly carrots'. The Greek philosopher Theophrastus (*c.*371-*c.*287 BC) describes silphium as thick-rooted with black bark, roughly 48 centimetres long, with a hollow fennel-like stalk and golden leaves like celery. The ancient physician Soranus recommended ingesting a chickpea-sized dose of it monthly to prevent pregnancy, and 'destroy any existing'. Whether it was through over-harvesting, or the desertification of ancient Cyrenaica (eastern Libya today), the plant died out,

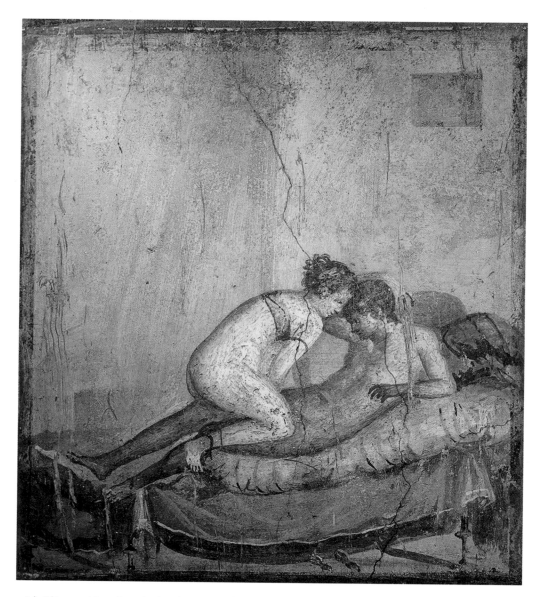

with Pliny writing that the last known stalk of Cyrenaican silphium was presented to Emperor Nero 'as a curiosity'.

All of this does, admittedly, paint the ancient Roman world as a singularly, carnivorously lustful time and place. But for the Roman interested more in the intellectual and sentimental approaches to relationships, comprehensive guides like the *Ars amatoria* ('The Art of Love'), an instructional series of three volumes by the Roman poet Ovid (43 BC–

A Roman fresco of a couple having sex, painted on the wall of the bedroom (Cubiculum) in the Casa del Centenario (IX 8,3) in Pompeii. First century.

AD 17/18), came to the rescue. Written in AD 2, the books are divided into intended audiences: Book One shows a man how to find a woman; Book Two shows him how to keep her. The advice could have been written yesterday – sections include 'not forgetting her birthday', 'letting her miss you, but not for long', and 'not

Another fresco of an erotic scene kept at the Gabinetto Segreto *(Secret Cabinet, or Museum), Naples.*

asking about her age'. The third book, which came two years after the first two, offers advice to women on how to keep a man. 'I have just armed the Greeks against the Amazons', wrote Ovid. 'Now, Penthesilea, it remains for me to arm thee against the Greeks …'

The Greek reference seems most apt, as the more famous Roman love stories of antiquity so often ended tragically. Most famous of these must be that of the Roman politician and general Mark Antony and Cleopatra VII Philopator (Cleopatra the father-beloved),

Queen of the Ptolemaic Kingdom of Egypt from 51 to 30 BC, and its last active ruler. The love affair persisted despite Antony marrying Octavia, sister of Caesar Augustus, to avert civil war in 40 BC, and resulted in three children: Alexander Helios, Cleopatra Selene II and Ptolemy Philadelphus. The hostility between Antony and Augustus erupted into civil war in 31 BC, with the Roman Senate

A depiction of Hermes with an enormous phallus, an apotropaic figure designed to frighten away evil.

waging war on Cleopatra and denouncing Antony a traitor. The couple eventually fled to Egypt where they suffered defeat at the Battle of Alexandria. Believing Cleopatra to have already taken her life, Antony ran himself through with his own sword; however, his friends brought him to a monument in which she was hiding, and he died in her arms. Cleopatra took her own life shortly after.

Around one hundred years later, there is the story of Hadrian and Antinous. While relationships between men were a part of Roman and Greek life, the affection that the Roman emperor Hadrian had for the younger Antinous, who was born to a Greek family near Claudiopolis (now north-west Turkey), seems to have been especially deep. Hadrian's marriage to Vibia Sabina (AD83-136/7), his second cousin once removed, was an unhappy one, perhaps informed by the early evidence of his same-sex attraction. At some point

Marble busts of the emperor Hadrian
(left, AD 125-130) and Antinous (right, AD 130-140).

Antinous became Hadrian's most favoured companion, and the two travelled throughout Italy, Asia Minor and North Africa, indulging in their shared love of hunting. In September 130 they killed a Marousian lion that had been attacking the local people, an episode that Hadrian then celebrated with bronze medallions and by commissioning historians and the poet Pancrates to write of it. The next record we

have of Antinous is in October 130, when he is reported to have died in the Nile, falling from Hadrian's flotilla. Death by drowning, it is assumed, though there have been theories that it was an assassination plotted by those at court, or even by Hadrian himself, who was known to have unpredictable fits of rage. Regardless, Hadrian was devastated by his death, with his biographer Aelius Spartianus attesting that he 'wept like a woman'. A distraught Hadrian founded a new city, Antinoöpolis, at the site of his death, and Antinous was venerated as the god Osiris-Antinous.

Graeco-Roman Amulets, Pilgrim Badges, and the Winged Phallus

There is no shortage of strange objects found by archaeologists and mudlarkers (amateur enthusiasts) who dig through and scavenge the river mud of Europe's waterways. But the objects shown here are of a kind that is perhaps the strangest and most enigmatic, and certainly the most eye-catching. From the Schelde Estuary of the Netherlands, from the banks of the Seine in Paris and from London's River Thames, a large, varying collection of these small leaden badges has been collected around Europe, with examples dating from the mid-fourteenth through to the early sixteenth century. The iconography varies wildly but is always comical and characterful, as is the (relatively scant) scholarship on the subject. The first badge shown here for example at the top of the page, showing a vagina riding a horse and brandishing a crossbow, is referred to by academics as 'Pussy Goes a Hunting'. The badge to the left of it shows a phallus with legs (referred to by scholars as an 'ambulant penis'), atop which stands a woman pushing a wheelbarrow full of miniature phalli, while the third badge shows a confrontation between an ambulant phallus and an ambulant vagina.

There are many, many others. On a good day a fortuitous mudlarker might perhaps stumble across 'ambulant vagina turning a phallus on a roasting spit'; 'phallus manning sailing vessel'; 'ambulant vagina on stilts with a crown of phalli'; or 'vagina climbing a ladder', to name but a few. But what – you might ask quite reasonably – the hell is going on here? There is no mention of these badges in contemporary literature, and so only the badges themselves can explain. Victorian scholars kept a wide berth from their pornographic appearance, while later examiners have variously described them as erotic and obscene. Theories abound. Were they bawdy gifts exchanged by sniggering lovers? Were they used to advertise one's sexual promiscuity? Symbols of fertility? Perhaps they were simply a product of a healthy tourist industry, where pedlars would sell similar badges of saints at sites of worship to those

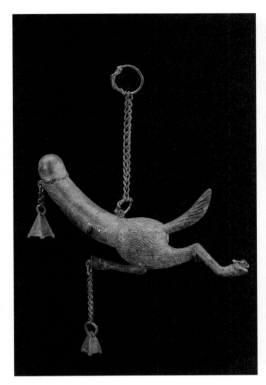

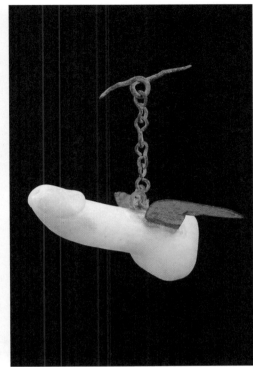

A likely influence on the medieval phallic badges are solid bronze Graeco-Roman amulets such as these. Top Left, one in the form of a phallus with the hindquarters of a horse, suspended by a chain with pendants attached at base. Top Right, a carved white alabaster phallus with bronze wings, made in Rome, Italy, c.100 BC-AD 100. Right, another with equine hindquarters, this one mounted by a female figure, c.100 BC-AD 400.

making pilgrimage, for one to wear proudly as a badge of virtue on one's chest and perhaps absorb some of the saint's healing power.

With such comically exaggerated scenes of lust and eroticism the leading theory is that these amulets are 'apotropaic' devices, used to defend oneself from the 'evil eye' and other supernatural agents of malice. Their ridiculous appearance distracts attention away from the wearer, and the happy laughter that the badges provoked wherever they were worn was another positive energy to ward off negative influences. Centuries later, the effect (for some, at least) remains the same!

Opposite: The extraordinary fresco known as the Albero della Fecondità *(Fertility Tree, known locally as the Penis Tree), created in 1265 but only discovered in 1999 in the street-level* loggia *(balcony) of a thirteenth-century former wheat store in the Italian town of Massa Marittima. Eight female figures are gathered below the tree and its fruit of twenty-five penises, apparently hitting the branches with sticks and fighting over the fallen fruit. The symbolism is debated, but one theory is that this represents the contemporary notion in Tuscan folklore that was later recorded in the notorious witchfinder's guide, the* Malleus Maleficarum *(Hammer of the Witches). The book notes that when looking to identify a witch, look for someone stealing male genitalia and keeping them alive in bird's nests.*

Above Left and Right: A woman riding a bird-legged phallus on a moonlit night; and a flying phallus copulating with a flying vagina. Two gouache paintings thought to have been made in India, c.1900 in the collection of the Wellcome Library, which have otherwise baffled their cataloguers.

The Kama Sutra

Though it was written in Sanskrit by the Indian philosopher known as Vatsyayana sometime in the second or third century, English readers were only able to buy a published translation of the *Kama Sutra* in 1963. This was shortly after the landmark 'Chatterley trial' of 1960, when Penguin Books were cleared of obscenity charges for publishing D. H. Lawrence's *Lady Chatterley's Lover*. In fact, an English translation had first appeared in 1883 by Sir Richard Francis Burton (1821-90), though less well known is the fact that the lion's share of the work had actually been done by his friend and colleague Forster Fitzgerald Arbuthnot (1833-1901), along with the Indian archaeologist Bhagwan Lal Indraji and a student named Shivaram Parshuram Bhide.

This translation was privately printed, and soon became one of the most pirated publications of the Victorian era because of its reputation – just as we popularly think of it today – as an erotic guide to sex. But this is a gross misconception, as the discussion of sex positions and related gymnastics of the intimate art is only one part of Vatsyayana's writings on Kama. This is defined as the enjoyment of experiences through the five

A Kama decoration carved on the walls of the Lakshmana (or Lakshman) Temple in Khajuraho, Madhya Pradesh, India, tenth century.

A Kama carving at the royal palace of Kathmandu, which dates back to the Licchavi period (fourth to eighth century).

An ancient sculpture of sexual behaviour in the wall of Umamaheshwor Temple at Kritipur.

discusses the lifestyle and goals of a *nagarika* (or city-dweller) and the characteristics of different types of women. Part II delves into the practicality of sexual union, but Part III then veers towards advice on acquiring a wife, and Part IV on family life. But it is the advice on 'embraces', and then 'unions', to which most readers hastily thumb, which begins with the distinguishing of types of lover. 'Man is divided into three classes,' writes Burton in his translation. 'Viz. the hare man, the bull man, and the horse man, according to the size of his *lingam*. Woman also, according to the depth of her *yoni*, is either a female deer, a mare, or a female elephant.' (Vatsyayana didn't actually use *lingam* and *yoni*, these are Burton's own deployments in order to lessen outrage.) Types of embrace are listed, including 'Jataveshtitaka, or the twining of the creeper' and 'Vrikshadhirudhaka, or climbing a tree', which are both embraces while standing up. 'Tila-Tandulaka, or the mixture of sesamum seed with rice' is when lovers lie in bed and embrace very closely with limbs rubbing against each other, while 'Kshiraniraka, or milk and water embrace' is when a woman sits on the lap of the man.

The next is 'On Kissing', which has guidance like: 'when one of them takes both the lips of the other between his or her own, it is called a "clasping kiss". A woman, however, only takes this kind of kiss from a man who has no moustache.' In the chapter 'On Biting, and the Means to be Employed with Regard to Women of Different Countries', it is advised that: 'All the places that can be kissed are also the places that can be bitten, except the upper lip, the interior of the mouth, and the eyes.' And then most famously there is the chapter 'Of the Different Ways of Lying Down, and Various Kinds of Congress'. Positions listed include 'the yawning position … when she raises her thighs and keeps them wide apart

senses, assisted by the mind together with the soul. In the context of the Sutra, this covers every aspect of the relationship between a man and woman: education, courtship, marriage and conjugal life. As Vatsyayana explains at the end of the text: 'A person acquainted with the true principles of this science, who preserves his Dharma (virtue or religious merit), his Artha (worldly wealth) and his Kama (pleasure or sensual gratification), and who has regard to the customs of the people, is sure to obtain the mastery over his senses. In short, an intelligent and knowing person attending to Dharma and Artha and also to Kama, without becoming the slave of his passions, will obtain success in everything that he may do.'

The first part of the *Kama Sutra* doesn't in fact have anything to do with sex but

and engages in congress'. The clasping position 'when the legs of both the male and female are stretched straight out over each other'. When the woman places one leg on her lover's head while stretching the other out, it's known as 'the fixing of the nail', but if she then alternates the leg positions, it's called 'the splitting of the bamboo'. 'When both the legs of the woman are contracted, and placed on her stomach, it is called the "crab's position".' The Sutra reports

Opposite: Lovers embracing, from an erotic Indian manuscript of c.1660.

Right: A vignette from the margins of a leaf from a fifteenth-century French Book of Hours. Whether it shows the influence of the Kama Sutra, or whether it's merely the satirical doodle of a bored scribe, it is still startling to see. Especially given the fact that the central illumination of the folio, just above this image, is of the Virgin Mary carrying the infant Christ on a donkey.

that the writer Suvarnanabha recommends practising these in water to make it easier, but Vatsyayana disapproves of this as it is prohibited by religious law. Some other choice tips include: 'When a woman stands on her hands and feet like a quadruped, and her lover mounts her like a bull, it is called the "congress of the cow".' 'When a man enjoys two women at the same time … it is called the "united congress". When a man enjoys many women altogether, it is called the "congress of a herd of cows".'

Vatsyayana's writing is notable for his focus on providing as much practical instruction for women as men, advising on their wifely duties and the secrets to maintaining conjugal happiness. He also makes recommendations of sixty-four arts that women should study, which include cookery, dressmaking and perfumery, and less expected suggestions like conjuring, chess, bookbinding and carpentry. Number forty-five is *mlecchita-vikalpa*, the art of code-writing, which women can use to help keep liaisons a secret. Other practical advice includes avoiding prospective lovers that have worms in their stool, or whose breath 'smells of crows'. Women should feel free to manipulate men for money and goods, and if the man is no longer able or willing to provide these, then he should be discarded. Ways to alienate this useless man include 'curling the lip in a sneer', 'stamping on the ground' and 'ignoring him'.

She could also psychologically belittle him by discussing subjects about which he knows little, show contempt for the things he does know about, deliberately distort his meaning, laugh when he says something sincere and laugh about something else when he makes a joke. She can also discuss his bad habits and vices in public.

Not all the tips are winners, of course. Of all of them, it's probably best to ignore the recommendation to smear one's 'instrument' in honey, powdered thorn apple and black pepper to 'induce ecstasy'.

Lady Xoc's Carved Tongue-Piercing Lintel (c.726) – Love in Mesoamerica

In this stunning carved lintel we find Lady Xoc, Maya queen consort of King Shield Jaguar II, kneeling before her adoring husband and pulling a rope pierced with obsidian razorblades through her tongue, causing her blood to pour into the offering bowl on the ground. In the iconography of the Maya it is extremely rare to see a female figure perform such an important ritual, in this case a sacrificial bloodletting which nobles believed allowed them to communicate with their gods and ancestors. (Although with a spiked rope through one's tongue one would expect coherent conversation to have been a challenge.) The text at the head of the panel informs us that this event took place in October in the year 709, and traces of pigment tell us that the carving would have been even more striking in its original state, as it was painted in bright red and blue. This particular lintel adorns an uncovered Maya building referred to by archaeologists as

'Structure 23', which appears to have been built by King Shield Jaguar as a romantic gift for his wife, as a place for her and her ladies of court to convene. Through this loving act of homage to his wife, Structure 23 and the lintels that decorate it have taught us much about the role of women in Maya politics.

Blood was one substance at the heart of Maya life; another was cocoa. In fact, in situations where bloodletting would be inconvenient, chocolate sourced from their landscape of cacao trees was dyed with red achiote paste and used to symbolise a sacrificial victim's blood in rituals. The significance of this is why we find chocolate integral to Maya marriage ceremonies. The father of the intended bride would invite the prospective groom for a discussion of his proposal over a cup of cocoa. At the wedding day, the bride and groom would exchange five grains of cacao with each other, while their guests would 'chokola'j' – drink chocolate together.

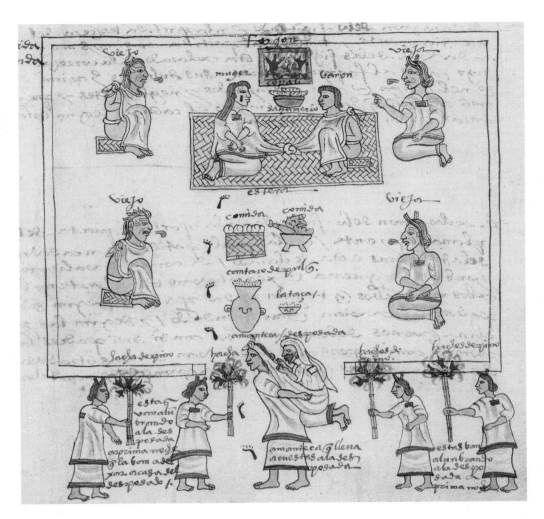

An Aztec wedding ceremony.

The Aztecs placed the same importance on cocoa as the Maya. Excessive consumption of the drink was even credited as being the secret to the Aztec emperor Motecuhzoma Xocoyotzin's success with women. Dowries were often paid in, and sex often paid for, with cocoa; and Aztec weddings were equally chocolatey affairs. Wonderfully, we can actually examine a scene of Aztec marriage in one of the illustrated pages contained in the Codex Mendoza, a manuscript recounting the history of the Aztecs thought to have been created in 1541.

The image, shown here, reveals the stages of the ritual, beginning at the bottom of the page (other details are filled in by another manuscript called the Florentine Codex). The night-time ceremony was initiated by the torch-lit arrival of the bride (who was usually fifteen years of age) at the groom's house, carried on the back of the person who had arranged the matching of the young couple. A feast of ground maize, tamales and a bowl of turkey heads and drumsticks was arranged for the guests, who can be seen in the picture offering advice from their seats, as they get steadily drunker on pulque, the fermented juice of the maguey plant. In the centre at the

top of the image the new husband and wife are literally tying the knot, their clothes bound together symbolically.[1] The ritual now complete, the pair are then led to their bedchamber. There they are left alone to consummate the union for an exhausting four days, with only periodic breaks for meals of chocolate, tamales and turkey heads to recharge, before settling into newly wedded life.

A scene of a Mixtec (a separate pre-Columbian culture) wedding ceremony that took place in 957 BC in our Gregorian calendar, between the bride Three Flint and groom Twelve Wind, painted on the deer-skin pages of the Codex Zouche-Nuttall. In the centre the couple can be seen consummating their marriage.

---

1 This is of course not the origin of the English phrase 'tying the knot' but is just one example of metaphorical tethering that is most common in the form of 'handfasting'. The ritual of tying the hands of a couple can be found anywhere from Hindu Vedic communities to the Celts in Scotland, where lovers were bound with a knotted cord.

Right: The Moche civilisation of northern Peru flourished from c.100 to 800. This Moche ceremonial vessel represents the belief in the sexually active, living cadavers of the underworld. The exaggerated proportions emphasise his ability to masturbate and produce semen to fertilise the living earth.

Below: A detail of another Mixtec marriage scene, this time between Lord Eight Deer Jaguar Claw and Lady Thirteen Serpent, who exchange a cup of cocoa. Lord Eight Deer Jaguar Claw (1063-1115) was a powerful Mixtec ruler in eleventh-century Oaxaca and relentlessly power-hungry. The Codices reveal that he arranged for himself several marriages into different Mixtec royal lineages as a strategy to achieve sovereignty.

Norse Brooch (800-900) —
A Viking Guide to Dating

We don't commonly associate the Vikings with the lighter and more emotional aspects of the human experience. Even their ideas for relaxation sound brutal. From the Icelandic sagas we learn various details of what they did for pleasure, like the game *hnútukast*, in which one attempted to kill an opponent by hurling bones at their head as hard as possible. *Sköfuleikr* was pretty to similar to *hnútukast*, except that you threw pot scrapers made from cow horn; *sund* was a kind of underwater wrestling in which you tried to drown your friend; and there was also a form of tug of war played over an open fire, in which you both stood naked and tugged on an animal skin to try and pull your opponent into the flames.

A Norse brooch fashioned c.800-900, with astonishingly fine filigree and granulation, found as part of a hoard at Hornelund, Denmark, and considered one of the finest survivals of the Viking culture. Likely commissioned as a wedding gift by a groom looking to impress his bride and advertise his wealth and status.

All of which makes it hard to believe there was much time left for gentler romantic endeavours, but archaeological relics and the sagas do shed some light on this aspect of daily life. Marriages were a way to forge alliances, with the families of the bride and groom conducting the negotiations, but appropriate courtship was important to help catalyse the union. Cultivating what the Norse called *inn matki munr* ('the mighty passion') was a delicate art. Take too long to make an advance to your betrothed, or conduct it too lackadaisically, and you risked insulting the bride's family. Eighteen separate courtships mentioned in the sagas end bloodily because of this lacklustre engagement. Equally dangerous was moving too fast and causing a pre-marital

pregnancy. There were traditions to observe – the bride-to-be could signal her approval by making her mate a shirt. The groom-to-be, on the other hand, could pay no better compliment than picking a bouquet of purple flowers and – in accordance with the custom – slapping her in the face with it.

Marriage was viewed as essential for the survival of society, and singletons risked being outcast. Any bachelor dragging his heels was accused of 'fleeing from the vagina', while potential spinsters were 'fleeing from the penis'.

Before the arrival of Christianity, Norse views on homosexuality were complicated but largely tolerant. Although there is no mention of attitudes to lesbianism, men could conduct sexual relationships with other men so long as it didn't interfere with their marriage. As long as he performed his husbandly duties, then his wife and her family would tolerate his male bedroom companions.

When it comes to sex scenes in the sagas, the language is quite decorous, the initiation alluded to with phrasing like the man 'turning towards' her, 'laying his hand [or arm or thigh] on her'. The reader then had to fill in the gap with their own imagination. Couples in coitus are described as 'crowding together in bed', with the man in the peak throes 'romping on her belly', and the couple said to be 'travelling together'. When they were done the pair would enjoy *hvila meth henna* (rest with her), or the man would 'amuse one's self', which believe it or not refers to him having a quiet conversation or playing a game of cards.

Old Norse sex slang can be found still littering the cruder corners of the English language today. *Thviet*, meaning a cut or slit, is the root of the Old English *thwat*, from which the 'h' would later be dropped for the modern insult. The Norse word for female genitals, *kunta*, also lingers.

While it was ideal for the bride to be a virgin, it was not required for marriage; and for the man there was no such restriction on sex before, or even outside of, marriage, as long as no children were produced out of wedlock. Any that were born became the responsibility of the woman's family,

Scandinavia's only surviving silver figure of Freyja, goddess of love and seduction, found at Tissø, Denmark.

while the birth was also likely to prevent any man in the future taking the mother as his bride. As well as the permitted adultery with other Norse women, men were allowed 'frilles', or lower-class women who served as concubines, and 'bed slaves', with whom consent was less of a factor. If the experience of the latter wasn't bad enough, after the death of their captor these slaves often found themselves sacrificed as part of his funereal ritual, as witnessed by the Arab explorer Ahmad Ibn Fadlān (*c.*879-960), who described in terrible detail one such ceremony memorialising a Viking chieftain that horrified him. All of this was permitted for the male Norseman. However, touch another man's wife, and you were likely to find yourself fined or executed.

Fair Rosamund – *Henry II and the Secret in the Labyrinth* (c.1166)

The real, and legendary, details of the life of Rosamund Clifford (born before 1140 – died 1175/6) make up a tragic romance that is woven in the fabric of medieval British history, embellished by compilers of colourful historical chronicles and inspiring artists and poets for centuries. The story has it all: an extraordinarily beautiful mistress to a king, a murderously jealous queen, an elaborately disguised secret affair, and a violently bloody end. But how much tangible fact is there in the fog of fiction?

It begins, as so many grim episodes of history do, with a king's wandering eye. Henry II (1133-89), first English king of the House of Plantagenet, married Eleanor of Aquitaine in 1152. This union with the heiress to the House of Poitiers helped to secure a kingdom that comprised the whole of England, most of Wales, the eastern half of Ireland and the western half of France, and together Henry and Eleanor had eight children. His was an energetic reign notable for restoring royal administration in England, laying the basis for English Common Law and expanding the French arm of his empire by pushing east and south, in a 'cold war' with Louis VII.

Rosamund, a reputed beauty, is assumed to have been the daughter of the noble Marcher lord (a precursor to the title Marquess) Walter de Clifford (1113-90). We know nothing of her childhood, nor the circumstances or date of when she met the king, but at some point in the 1160s Henry and Rosamund began an affair. According to legend, it began in 1166 when Eleanor was pregnant with their eighth child, John. If it did indeed begin this early then the relationship was kept well under wraps, as the king only publicly acknowledged the affair in 1174.

Rosamund was said to have been sequestered away at Woodstock Palace, Henry's favourite retreat, where an adjoining building called Everswell was constructed with a complex design of pools, a cloister, an orchard, bower and pleasure garden, according to a later sketch made by John Aubrey in the seventeenth century. A spring there was later named 'Rosamund's Well'. This seems to show the romantic influence of the chivalric tale of Tristan and Isolde, in which the pair secretly meet in an orchard and pass messages to each other by dropping twigs into the stream that runs through her chamber.

Opposite: Fair Rosamund *(1861), a portrait by Dante Gabriel Rossetti (1828-82).*

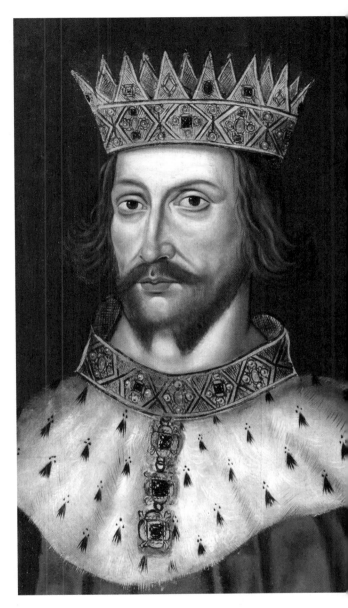

Portrait of King Henry II of England by an unknown artist (c.1597-c.1618).

Meanwhile, Eleanor gave birth to John in Beaumount Palace instead of at Woodstock Palace, because of Rosamund's presence there.

Gerald of Wales, writing with scathing wordplay just before 1200, records how Henry imprisoned Eleanor for turning their children against him, and 'having long been a secret adulterer, now openly flaunted his mistress, not that rose of the world [*rosa-mundi*] of false and frivolous renown, but that rose of unchastity [*rosa-immundi*]' (*Gir. Camb. opera*, 4.21-2). In just her second year of living openly as the king's mistress, however, Rosamund died unexpectedly around 1176, and was buried at Godstow Abbey. Her tomb was elaborately decorated. In 1191, Hugh, Bishop of Lincoln, visited the Abbey and to his horror found Rosamund buried in a spectacular tomb covered with hangings, lamps and wax candles at pride-of-place inside the church before the front of the high altar. Deeming this profane, he had her reburied outside, supposedly in the chapter house, where her tomb had the inscription:

This tomb doth here enclose the world's
  most beauteous Rose,
Rose passing sweet erewhile, now nought
  but odour vile.

As the years passed, the story of the royal mistress who died too soon entered into folklore and became as lavishly garnished as her tomb. In the sixteenth and early seventeenth centuries, the story became that Henry had constructed a complicated labyrinth at Woodstock, at the centre of which he would hold his secret trysts with Rosamund. Eleanor eventually discovered their affair, using a thread to guide her to the centre of the maze where she found the pair. One version of the legend tells of the queen as later confronting Rosamund with a choice: die by drinking from a poisoned bowl or die by the dagger. Rosamund chose the former. Another version has it that Eleanor ordered Rosamund to be burned between two fires, stabbed and left to bleed out in a bath of boiling water. All of which seems most unlikely, given that Eleanor was by this time languishing in prison for having inspired her sons to rebel against their father – but let's not let facts get in the way of a good legend.

Above: The ruins of Godstow Abbey, Oxfordshire. Somewhere in the grounds lies the lost grave of Rosamund Clifford.

Opposite: Queen Eleanor *(1858) by Frederick Sandys (1829-1904), clutching the poisoned chalice in one hand, and in the other the dagger, and the red thread she used to find her way to Rosamund's bower at the centre of the maze.*

The Rosa Celestial – *Dante and Beatrice*

The figures of Dante and Beatrice stare up at the Rosa Celestial in Gustave Doré's illustration of Canto XXXI of the *Paradiso*, marvelling at the heavenly rings of the angel hierarchy, just before Saint Bernard of Clairvaux takes Beatrice's place as Dante's guide in the next canto:

That sacred army, that Christ espoused with his blood, displayed itself in the form of a white rose, but the Angel other, that sees and sings the glory, of him who inspires it with love, as it flies, and sings the excellence that has made it as it is, descended continually into the great flower, lovely with so many petals, and climbed again to where its love lives ever, like a swarm of bees, that now plunges into the flowers, and now returns, to where their labour is turned to sweetness.

When we think of Dante Alighieri (*c.*1265-1321), we think also of Beatrice. The two names are as securely coupled in popular consciousness as Justinian and Theodora, Tristan and Isolde, Lancelot and Guinevere. It might be surprising, then, to learn the details of their real-life relationship. Or, more accurately, the lack of one. Though she would be the principal inspiration for Dante's *Vita Nuova* (1294) and appear as a symbol of divine grace and theology in the *Divine Comedy* (written between *c.*1308 and 1320), in reality – according to Dante – he and Beatrice met only twice.

The two encounters took place nine years apart. The first was when Dante's father, Alighiero di Bellincione (*c.*1210-83), brought him to a May Day party at her family's house.

Even though they were both nine years old at the time, Dante recalled falling in love with Beatrice 'at first sight', apparently without even speaking to her, and was from that moment unable to forget her for the rest of his life.[1] The consensus among scholars is that Beatrice is Beatrice Portinari (1265-90), daughter of a Florentine banker, who would go on to marry the banker Simone de' Bardi in 1287. Dante, meanwhile, married Gemma Donati (*c.*1267-after 1333), fulfilling an engagement that had been arranged when he was twelve years old. Their next meeting was even briefer, a chance encounter in the streets of Florence. Dante spied Beatrice in a white dress, flanked by two older women, walking towards him. Beatrice recognised him and called out a greeting, but Dante was so flustered by this that he couldn't speak and ran away.[2]

That was apparently the last the two saw of each other. Seven years later, at the age

---

1 Which calls to mind a quote from Clive James's *Unreliable Memoirs* (1980), about the imprint of his own fleeting childhood love: 'Even though I can't bring back her face,' he writes, 'I can recall exactly the sensation of beatitude. We forget the shape of the light but remain dazzled for ever.'

2 Beatrice's greeting in the street inspired a dramatic erotic vision in Dante, that he wrote into a sonnet and sent to poet friends appealing for their interpretation. In it, the Lord of Love appeared to him. He held Beatrice in his arms, wearing only a crimson cloth, and fed her his burning heart. Friends wrote back to him with their thoughts, including one who advised Dante to 'give your balls/a good wash, so that the vapours/that make you talk nonsense/are extinguished and dispersed'. Dante grumbled that 'no one understood the true meaning of my dream'.

Opposite: Gustave Doré's (1832-83) illustration of the Rosa Celestial of Paradiso, *the third and final part of Dante's* Divine Comedy. *This is the Empyrean, the highest heaven, and dwelling place of God.*

of twenty-five, Beatrice's death is recorded. Dante withdrew from society and threw himself into preserving her, or his idealised version of her, in poems, and three years later these were published in the form of *Vita Nuova* (New Life). This is very much in the medieval literary tradition of 'courtly love', in which a writer or artist conducted a secret and unrequited admiration for a noble lady, often without ever meeting the object of their artistic attention. The women were usually not even aware of their role as muse.

The British Pre-Raphaelite painter Henry Holiday's (1839-1927) imagining of the scene of Dante and Beatrice passing each other in the streets of Florence. Holiday travelled to Florence for research, painstakingly including details like the scaffolding surrounding the Ponte Vecchio, which was being rebuilt after flooding at the time.

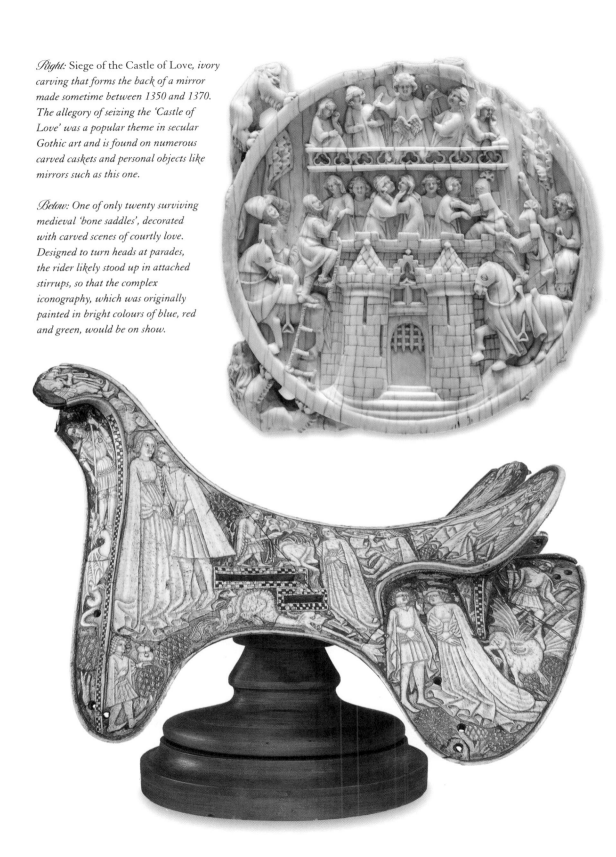

Right: Siege of the Castle of Love, *ivory carving that forms the back of a mirror made sometime between 1350 and 1370. The allegory of seizing the 'Castle of Love' was a popular theme in secular Gothic art and is found on numerous carved caskets and personal objects like mirrors such as this one.*

Below: One of only twenty surviving medieval 'bone saddles', decorated with carved scenes of courtly love. Designed to turn heads at parades, the rider likely stood up in attached stirrups, so that the complex iconography, which was originally painted in bright colours of blue, red and green, would be on show.

Jeanne de Clisson's My Revenge *(1343-59)*

Approximately 150 manuscript copies survive of Jean Froissart's *Chronicles*, a gargantuan fourteenth-century prose history of the brutal Hundred Years' War. Illustrated copies are not for the squeamish; bloody battle scenes aside, there are also skilful miniatures of notable episodes like the execution of Hugh the Younger Despenser (*c.*1287/1289), a murderous cheat who after being found guilty by Queen Isabella was, Froissart tells us, tied naked to a ladder in a public square, castrated, disembowelled, and had his heart cut out and thrown on a fire. See also the Ball of the Burning Men, a masquerade ball held for Charles VI of France on 28 January 1393 in Paris that went disastrously wrong when five French nobles performing a dance dressed in costume as 'wild men' caught fire, as the musicians kept playing. Four of the men burned to death, while the fifth survived by jumping into a vat of wine.

The illustration shown opposite is taken from the most lavishly illustrated version of Froissart's *Chronicles*, copied and illuminated in the first half of the 1470s in Bruges, Flanders, in modern Belgium. The scene is the execution of Olivier IV de Clisson (1300-43), a Breton Marche Lord and knight who in the conflict known as the War of the Breton Succession, had backed the Counts of Blois against the English-supported Montforts of Brittany for control of the Sovereign Duchy of Brittany. While defending the city of Vannes, De Clisson was captured by an English–Breton force but released for a surprisingly small ransom. This led to the suspicion that he had traitorously allowed the force to take the city. The next year, in 1343, he and fifteen other Norman lords were lured to a French tournament, believing themselves safe following the signing of the Truce of Malestroit between England and France. They were thrown in irons and brought to Paris for trial. De Clisson's wife, Jeanne de Clisson (1300-59), also known as Jeanne de Belleville, fought desperately for his release, and from records appears to have even bribed the King's Sergeant to 'hamper the execution', for which the man was arrested. To the shock of the nobility, Olivier IV de Clisson was executed by beheading at La Halles on 2 August 1343, despite the fact that no evidence of his guilt was ever demonstrated.

Not for a moment was concern given as to how the widow De Clisson would react to this bloody injustice, and certainly no one could have predicted the scale of what would ensue. Jeanne de Clisson was arrested for her bribery of the King's Sergeant, but she escaped. Boiling rage tempered her pain to steely determination, and she set about planning her revenge on the French king, Philip VI, and Charles de Blois, for what she saw as the cowardly murder of her beloved husband. She began building her own private war fund, selling the De Clisson property until enough money was raised to hire a force of 400 men. With her new loyal army, she began to savage the strongholds of French forces: first a castle at Touffou, outside Bignon, commanded by an officer of Charles de Blois who, upon

dic et le roy dangleterre a
non enfraindre. Comment
le roy de france fist decapi-
ter le sire de clicon z pluse
mrultres chrers de bretaigne
z de normādie. Le .C. chap

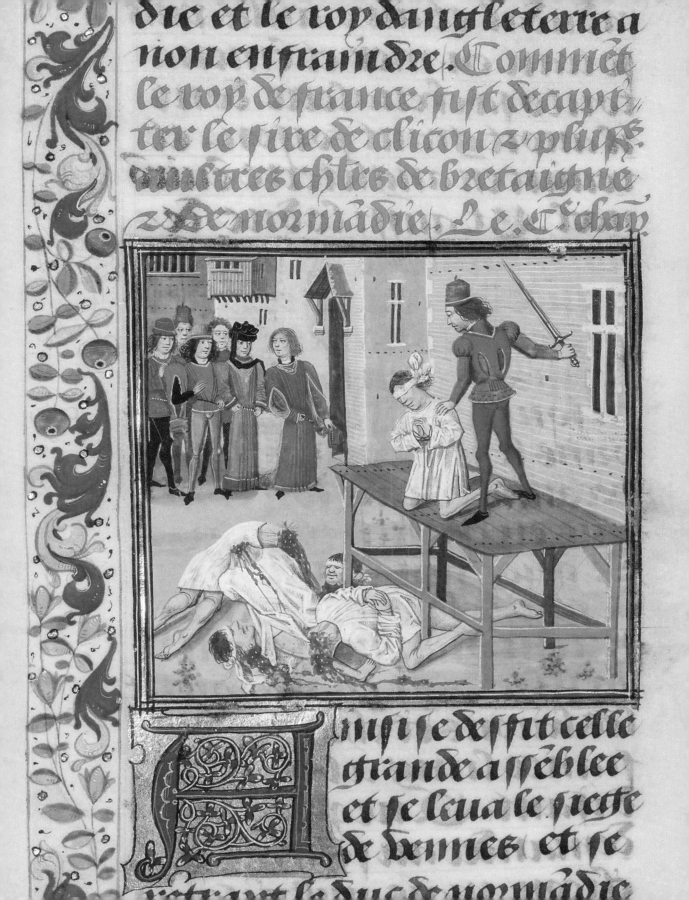

nsi se desfit celle
grande assemblee
et se leua le prelte
de vennes et se
retira le duc de normādie

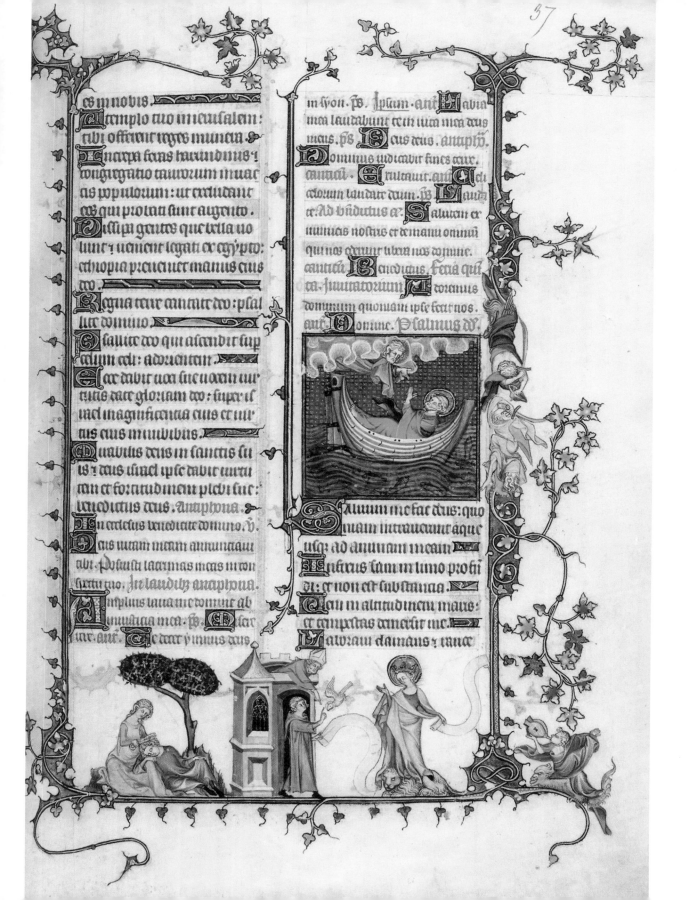

37

recognising Jeanne, politely allowed her entry. She and her men massacred the entire garrison, leaving one man to tell the story of what had happened. Then a garrison formerly under her husband's command at Château-Thébaud, south-east of Nantes, suffered the same fate. Further castles and garrisons were seized and looted, and chroniclers of the time note her unwavering lack of mercy in slaughtering whomever she found inside, though always leaving one survivor.

'The Bloody Lioness' of Brittany, as she was now known, then enlisted the help of Breton sympathisers and the English king, Edward III, in forming a corsair fleet of three warships painted black with red sails, with the flagship named 'My Revenge'. For nine months her Black Fleet terrorised the Kingdom of France, killing every French crew they encountered and sinking every ship, first in the Bay of Biscay and eventually in the English Channel, where they stalked French commercial vessels. Finally, ships dispatched by King Philip VI engaged and destroyed her fleet, although Jeanne and her son Olivier managed to escape and were

taken to safety in Morlaix, Brittany. Unfazed, she outfitted new vessels and maintained her piratical campaign for another thirteen years before settling into a peaceful retirement.

Peter I of Portugal and Inês de Castro (1361)

Titled *Le Couronnement d'Inès de Castro en 1361* (The Coronation of Inès de Castro in 1361), this oil on canvas by the French artist Pierre Charles Comte (1823-95) captures one of the strangest episodes in Portuguese history: the crowning of the wife of King Peter I of Portugal (1320-67). Peter stands beside Inês de Castro in a packed hall, overseeing the kneeling courtier paying homage to his queen. Nearly all eyes in the room are turned downwards – out of respect, one would assume, unless one knew the story unfolding here, which is hinted at by the woman's sunken, sallow skin. The averted gazes are more likely to be out of fear and disgust, for the hand that the courtier kisses is that of a corpse. At the time of her coronation in 1361, Inês de Castro had been dead for four years.

Peter and Inês had met in 1340, when at fifteen years old she was sent by her Castilian family to be lady-in-waiting to Peter's first wife, Constanza of Castile. Peter and Inês began an affair, and five years later, when Constanza died shortly after giving birth to Ferdinand I (future king of Portugal), Peter sought permission from his father King Alfonso IV to marry Inês. Alfonso deemed her unsuitable and banished her from the court, but the couple continued their relationship nevertheless, having four children between 1346 and 1354 at a villa outside Coimbra, a home that would be known as the Villa of Tears. King Alfonso, meanwhile, continued to worry that Inês would exert Castilian influence over his son, and so finally dispatched three assassins to murder her. The killers found her in the villa courtyard beside the fountain and butchered her.

A distraught Peter buried Inês at Coimbra's Monastery of Santa Clara-a-Velha. When he inherited the throne in 1357, following his father's death, Peter immediately sought revenge. Two of his wife's murderers were captured and brought before him, whereupon he ordered that their hearts be ripped out in front of him. He then revealed that he and Inês had, in fact, married in secret, which

Detail of the painting showing the corpse of Inês de Castro seated on the throne.

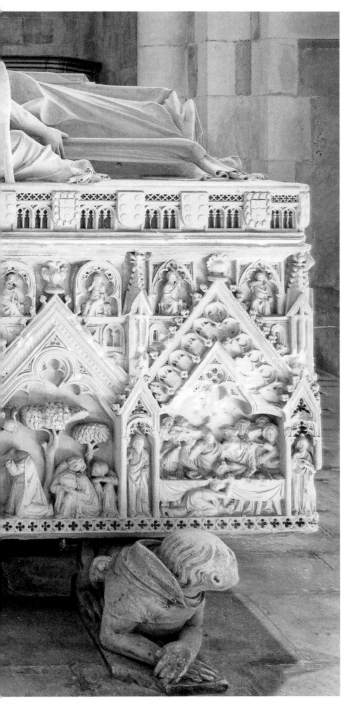

meant that she was now the rightful queen of Portugal, regardless of her cardiopulmonary status. (While some sources say Peter demanded the coronation of Inês take place during his own ceremony of 1357, this painting is tied to the alternative version of the story that her body was dug up and crowned in 1361.) The corpse of Inês de Castro was exhumed, dressed in royal robes and placed on the throne for the ceremony. The romantic gesture also had practical benefits to it, as it legitimised the children that the two had had together. Her body was then buried at the Alcobaça Monastery in a tomb carved with her effigy. Peter's tomb was built opposite, so that on the day of the Last Judgement, when all the dead are resurrected for admission to heaven, the two will meet again.

The exquisitely carved tomb of Portugal's posthumous queen, Inês de Castro.

Taj Mahal, the Samarkand Mosque, and Other Romantic Monuments *(fifteenth century)*

One of the most famous structures in the world hides a secret at its centre. Every
day, visitors to the gleaming white Taj Mahal mausoleum, on the bank of the river
Yamuna, file past the beautifully decorated sarcophagi of the Mughal emperor Shah
Jahan and his wife Mumtaz Mahal that lie beneath the huge vaulted 'onion' dome
that so famously distinguishes the monument. Most are unaware that these are
false sarcophagi, and that the real tombs of the emperor and the woman with whom
he was besotted, and in whose memory he had the entire complex constructed, are
actually situated a level below, where they are left to lie in peace together.

The reign of Shah Jahan (1592-1666), from
January 1628 until July 1658, is considered the
cultural golden age of Mughal, when artistic
and architectural achievements reached new
heights. The emperor's legacy is enshrined in

numerous buildings erected during his rule,
including the Pearl Mosque at Agra and the
new city at Delhi, which became his capital.
There is the huge fortress-palace complex
known as the Red Fort, the great mosque of

The actual tombs of Mumtaz Mahal (left) and Shah Jahan (right).

Jāmiʻ Masjid, the Shalimar gardens, the Mahabat Khan Mosque in Peshawar, and so on; but he entered global cultural memory with the commission of the Taj Mahal ('Crown of the Palace') in 1631. The building was designed to match in its scale the devastating loss of his third and favourite wife, Arjumand Banu (1593-1631), who was renamed Mumtaz Mahal ('the jewel of the palace') while giving birth to their fourteenth child. Until her death the two were described as inseparable. While renowned for her beauty, she was also considered a trusted advisor and was bestowed the imperial seal. According to the official court chronicler Motamid Khan in his *Iqbal Namah-e-Jahangiri*, this combination of beauty and intelligence eclipsed all others, and left the emperor with little interest in his relationship with his other wives, which 'had nothing more

than the status of marriage. The intimacy, deep affection, attention and favour which Shah Jahan had for Mumtaz exceeded what he felt for his other wives.'

The last eight years of the emperor's life were spent in confinement under house arrest at Agra Fort, imposed by his third son Aurangzeb who had defeated his brothers in a war of succession to seize power. Jahan's eldest daughter Jahanara Begum Sahib voluntarily shared her father's confinement in order to take care of him, until he eventually died on 30 January 1666 at the age of seventy-four. Aurangzeb agreed to allow Shah Jahan to be buried in the tomb beside Mumtaz Mahal. 'My father showed a great affection for my mother,' he wrote, 'so let his last resting place be close to hers.'

Less well known, though no less spectacular, is Bibi-Khanym Mosque at Samarkand, Uzbekistan, one of the most magnificent mosques of the Islamic world. In 1399 Saray Mulk Khanum (1343-1406), Empress of

The Bibi-Khanym Mosque at Samarkand.

Tamerlane and chief consort of Timur, ordered its construction while her husband was away at war, as a romantic surprise for his return. The greatest architects and artisans worked tirelessly on the project and in 1404 completed work on the Bibi-Khanym Mosque ('the Mosque of the Oldest Wife'). To this day you can find at the centre of its courtyard an extraordinary feature: an enormous, empty stone lectern measuring 7 feet 6 inches by 6 feet 6 inches (2.28m by 1.98m), upon which sat one of the oldest Qur'ans in the world, bound in gold and weighing around 300kg. The book had originally belonged to Osman (579-656), son-in-law to Muhammad, who was murdered while reading it, his blood spilling onto the pages and transforming it into a relic. A saint transported the ancient work to

Samarkand where it rested for centuries on this lectern, worshipped by locals and pilgrims. Popular belief held that the book could grant magical favours to those wishing to conceive – women wanting a son would circle the lectern three times, uttering prayers, in the hope of falling pregnant.

Above: The giant stone lectern at the fifteenth-century Bibi-Khanym Mosque at Samarkand, one of the most magnificent mosques of the Islamic world.

Opposite: The Albert Memorial, London, finished in 1876 after being commissioned by Queen Victoria in memory of her beloved husband Prince Albert, following his death in 1861. Though the most famous, it was not the first monument to Albert to be built. The Albert Memorial in Manchester, designed by Thomas Worthington, was the first to depict a seated Albert in 1865; while even earlier was the monument in his memory erected in Swanage in 1862, in the form of an obelisk.

The Sarcophagus Lid of Thanchvil Tarnai and Larth Tetnies; and Other Eternal Embraces

'When the earth shall claim your limbs, then shall you truly dance,' wrote the poet Khalil Gibran (1883-1931). Some of the most unusual and poignant discoveries made in archaeology have couples performing this dance of death together for all eternity. One of the most beautiful shared burials is the intimate scene sculpted in this Etruscan sarcophagus lid shown here, carved out of volcanic tuff at some point between 350 and 300 BC. A husband and wife lie on a bed with pillows, beneath crinkled sheets, in a loving embrace. As well as being a rare survival of a shared tomb of this period, the sarcophagus is simply a magnificent piece of art. Each of its sides bears detailed friezes of Greeks and Amazons, two lions sinking

their teeth into a bull as they drag it to the ground, cavalry and footsoldiers fighting, and a naked warrior in a hero's pose carrying a sword and shield in the centre of the action. But it's the carved couple on the lid that really takes the breath away, their shape being strikingly reminiscent of a human heart. An inscription tells us the tomb was made for Thanchvil Tarnai and her husband Larth Tetnies, son of Arnth Tetnies and Ramtha Vishnai.

Married couples are much more commonly featured in Etruscan art than in Greek traditions, as women played a more prominent role in rituals and public life. This we find supported in one of the great masterpieces of Etruscan funerary art known as the 'Sarcophagus of the Spouses' of 530-510 BC (shown opposite), in which a smiling couple banquet together, propped up on their elbows, with the husband's arm tenderly resting on his wife's shoulder. The sarcophagus is actually an urn designed to hold the remains of the deceased couple and was painstakingly

recomposed from 400 separate pieces before
being put on display at the National Etruscan
Museum of Villa Giulia, Rome.

It seems magical to find the same romantic
smile and casual, intimate hug between a
couple in the carving shown here, made
over 2,000 years before the Etruscan piece
on an entirely different continent. *The King's
Acquaintances Memi and Sabu* is a statue in
the collection of New York's Metropolitan
Museum of Art that's dated to the Egyptian
Old Kingdom *c.*2575-2465 BC by the style of
Sabu's haircut. Though details are scarce, it's
thought to be from the Memphite Region,
Giza, Western Cemetery, and an inscription
tells us that the pair are not royalty but royal
'acquaintances'. But the detail that makes it
truly extraordinary is in the carving itself,

Below: The terracotta Sarcophagus of
the Spouses, 530-510 BC, one of the great
masterpieces of Etruscan art.

Above: 'What will survive of us is love,' declared Philip Larkin in the poem 'An Arundel Tomb', written after visiting Chichester Cathedral with his lover Monica Jones in January 1956. The tomb chest (above) that so moved the poet features the figures of Richard Fitzalan (c.1313-76), Earl of Arundel, and his second wife, Eleanor of Lancaster (1318-72), lying hand in hand.

Left: Strikingly similar to the statue of Memi and Sabu is this carving of a seated couple of the Dogon peoples, made in West Africa in the eighteenth or early-nineteenth centuries. The piece is thought to be an elegant comment on the different, yet complementary, roles of the male and female partnership as a harmonious unit of life.

The tombs of J. W. C. van Gorcum and his wife J. C. P. H. van Aefferden, joined by hands across the dividing wall between Protestant and Catholic graveyards.

which is easy to miss at first. The most common pose of this type of statue is of the male figure stepping forward in a dominant manner; but here, Sabu returns her husband's embrace with her right hand wrapped around his waist, as they stand together side by side, equal. A memorial of a happy marriage, it would seem, between two people who lived over 4,500 years ago.

In England a famous carved tomb, shown opposite, continues this unusual idea of a pair embracing after death. It sits in Chichester

Cathedral and is believed to be the resting place of Richard Fitzalan, 10th Earl of Arundel (d. 1376) and his second wife, Eleanor of Lancaster (d. 1372). The male figure wears a warrior's suit of armour with the crest of the Fitzalan family, while the female figure wears a delicate veil, wimple and gown typical of the fourteenth century. The knight rests his feet on a lion, symbolising bravery, while his partner's feet are cushioned by a dog, symbolising loyalty. The man's right hand is ungloved, vulnerable, as he takes his wife's hand in his. On a visit to the cathedral the poet Philip Larkin was so struck by the husband and wife lying in their repose that he memorialised it with the poem 'An Arundel Tomb' (1956), which concludes:

The stone fidelity
They hardly meant has come to be
Their final blazon, and to prove
Our almost-instinct almost true:
What will survive of us is love

A remarkable pair of tombs in the Het Oude Kerkhof, Roermond, the Netherlands, shows how joined hands cross not just the boundary of death but also societal barriers too. When J. W. C. van Gorcum, a colonel of the Dutch Cavalry and militia commissioner in Limburg, died in 1880 after thirty-eight years of marriage, he was buried in the Protestant cemetery of the town in a tomb pressed against the perimeter wall. When his wife, J. C. P. H. van Aefferden, a Catholic, died eight years later, she left instructions to refuse her interment in the family tomb of the Catholic cemetery. Instead, she requested to be buried in a monument against the perimeter wall, directly opposite her husband's tomb on the other side, and have their resting places joined by the clasped hands shown in this photograph. 'Unable are the loved to die,' wrote Emily Dickinson. 'For love is immortality'.

Above: The Lovers of Cluj-Napoca, a pair of human skeletons holding hands for the last five thousand years, discovered in 2013 by archaeologists in the consecrated ground of the cemetery of a former Dominican convent in Cluj-Napoca, Romania. Both were around thirty years old at the time of their death and were buried facing each other, with hands interlocked. The male appears to have suffered a violent blow.

Opposite Top Left: The Hasanlu Lovers were found at the Teppe Hasanlu archaeological site in the West Azerbaijan Province of Iran in 1972. The two male skeletons apparently died together of asphyxiation around 800 BC.

Opposite Bottom Left: The two male skeletons known as The Lovers of Modena, found in 2009 by archaeologists in present-day Modena, Italy, with hands interlaced, and dating to between the fourth and sixth centuries.

Opposite Far Right: The Lovers of Valdaro, a pair of human skeletons thought to be approximately 6,000 years old. They were discovered in a 'lover's embrace' by archaeologists at a Neolithic tomb in San Giorgio near Mantua, Italy, in 2007.

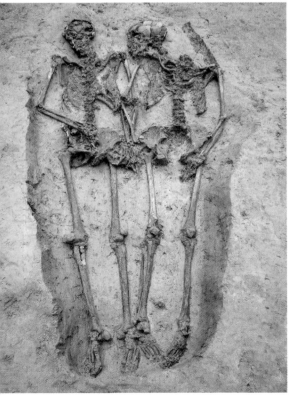

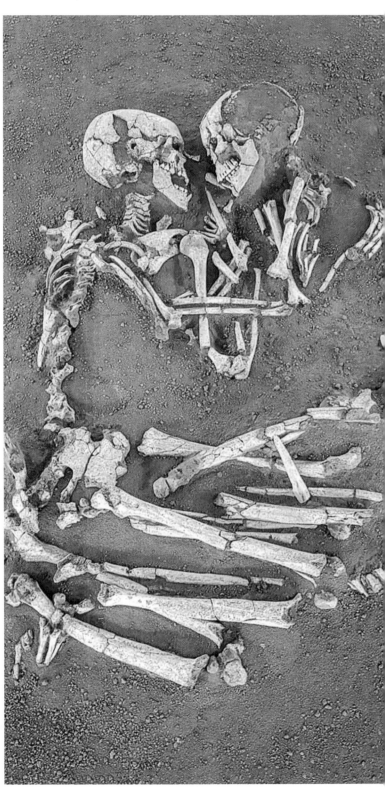

Jan van Eyck's
Arnolfini Portrait *(1434)*

Few paintings have been subjected to the same kind of obsessive scrutiny as the *Arnolfini Portrait* of 1434 by Jan van Eyck (*c*.1390-1441). It's a marital painting of a deceptive strangeness that slowly builds as one takes in the symbols and other clues scattered around the composition. Every single feature of this private room is a carefully selected component seemingly geared for the broadcast of one message: the wealth of the couple depicted. The intricate metalwork of the gleaming chandelier, the infamous convex mirror, the stained-glass window, the hint at a garden outside with a cherry tree. Fruit, a luxury item, is scattered casually on the sill and nearby chest, and light spills into a room rich in expensive fabrics draped over the luxurious carved furniture in a soft crimson that contrasts with the colours of the opulent furs, silks, velvets and wools clothing the couple. An oriental carpet lies on the floor.

But then we look closer, and more curious details, and questions, emerge. Religious symbols abound: the convex mirror is decorated with ten roundels containing scenes from Christ's Passion. The man's patten shoes in the lower left (and those of his companion behind them) are apparently a reference to a passage in the Book of Exodus 3:5: 'Put off thy shoes from thy feet, for the place whereon thou standest is holy ground.' An indication of a sacred event taking place? The chandelier has only one lit candle, the seeing eye of God. The mirror is unblemished, a traditional symbol of the purity of Mary, Mother of God. Rosary beads hang beside it. The oranges represent fertility, the cherry tree love. (While at first glance it appears that the woman is pregnant, she is, in fact, clutching the raised bulk of her dress in the manner of the period.) So, who are the figures seen here? We do not know for certain. In the earliest inventory record, the pallid man was identified as 'Hernoul le Fin', or 'Arnoult Fin' – this is probably the Bruges-based Italian merchant Giovanni di Nicolao di Arnolfini, who would have been the right

age at the time this painting was made. The woman is thought to be his undocumented second wife, whom he married after his first wife, Costanza Trenta, died in 1433. Recently the theory has been put forward that this is a posthumous portrait, begun when Costanza was alive, and finished a year after her death.

In 1934 the art historian Erwin Panofsky proposed the now-disputed idea that the painting served as a legal document of a marriage ceremony. The pose of the couple's hands appears reminiscent of taking vows in a marriage ceremony, and above the mirror we can see van Eyck's signature, more in the style of an official document than a painting: *Johannes de Eyck fuit hic. 1434* ('Jan van Eyck was here. 1434').

The most curious feature of all, though, is the convex mirror on the rear wall. It's a magnificent display of van Eyck's mastery of detail: the room is warped in perfect proportion in the mirror's reflection, which also reveals two figures standing opposite the couple, outside the frame of the painting, from our point of view. Could this be a slyly inserted self-portrait of van Eyck himself, arriving with his assistant through the doorway?

Above: The convex mirror detail of the portrait, showing two figures standing opposite the couple, one of whom is thought to be a self-portrait by van Eyck.

Opposite: For a more openly romantic marital painting there is The Honeysuckle Bower (c.1609), a self-portrait by the Flemish Baroque painter Peter Paul Rubens with his first wife Isabella Brant. The painting celebrates their wedding of 3 October 1609 and is replete with romantic symbolism – honeysuckle represented love and fidelity, the garden fertility, while the couple hold each other's right hand in union of marriage.

Hans Talhoffer's Fight Book (1459) — The History of the Husband-and-Wife Duel

A strange trend flourished in illustrated European fighting manuals of the fifteenth and early sixteenth centuries, as demonstrated by the wince-inducing illustrations shown here. These are vivid examples of a proposed solution to breakdowns in marital relations, taken from a *Fechtbuch* ('Fight Book') created in 1459 by Hans Talhoffer (*c.*1410 to 1415-*c.*1482), a German fencing expert and mercenary. The chapter provides information on the contemporary option available to husbands and wives, to resolve their disputes with a judicial duel, a Germanic legal custom invoked when no other legal recourse was available to settle an argument or effect a divorce.

The man's physical advantage is reduced by having him stand in a hole up to his waist, as the trial by combat plays out in a series of nine illustrations. The husband is armed with a sword, while the woman wields what appears to be a rock wrapped in a sheet as a kind of cudgel, and both are dressed in the same one-piece costume that covers the head. The series of images depicts the man, in his reduced position, being battered, bent over backwards and choked, face-gouged and put in a headlock. He manages to get in a few shots of his own, swiping at his wife's leg and at one point dragging her down headfirst into the hole with him. The caption of the final image, in which both contestants lie breathless and bleeding on the floor, translates as 'Here they make an end of each other.'

Paulus Kall, a defence master at the court of Bavaria, produced one of the earliest such fight manuscripts in 1400, with advice on fighting with daggers, swords, spades and stones, and how to conduct a marital duel. Beside a drawing of the husband standing in a hole, he describes the disadvantage the man faces: 'The woman must be so prepared that a sleeve of her chemise extend a small ell beyond her hand like a little sack. There indeed is put

a stone weighing three pounds; and she has nothing else but her chemise, and that is bound together between the legs with a lace. Then the man makes himself ready in the pit over against his wife. He is buried therein up to the girdle, and one hand is bound at the elbow to the side.'

The manuscripts written after Kall's works that mention these duels are thought to have simply copied his information, for the last recorded judicial duel between a husband and wife took place in Basel, Switzerland, at the same time that Kall wrote his manuscript in 1400. The dying-off of the practice is not thought to have been down to the easing of social attitudes towards women; rather, the opposite, as the historian Allison Coudert suggests: 'By the fifteenth and sixteenth centuries, law, custom, and religion were so stacked against aggressive and unruly wives that it is impossible to imagine civic authorities in any part of Europe condoning a wife's attack on her husband with a stone, much less a sword.'

With duelling out of the question, in England those in unhappy marriages had the option of the bizarre custom of wife-selling, which is thought to have sprung up in England in

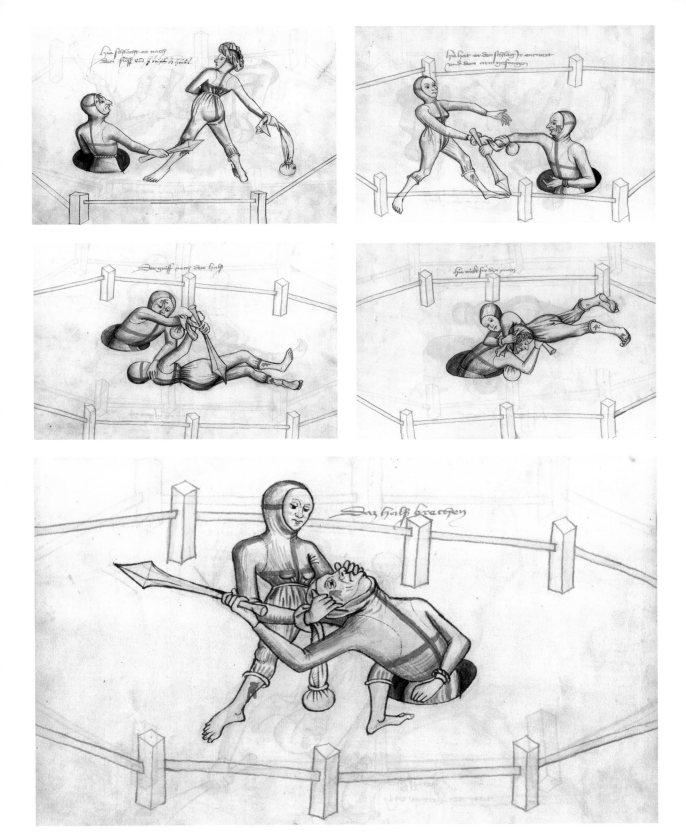

Opposite: A leaf from the 1523 fight-book manuscript of German fencing master Jörg Wilhalm Huter (1523-56). In the upper half, two bearded clergymen batter each other with spiked clubs; below, a wife takes great pleasure in preparing to pummel her husband with an improvised mace made from sheets.

Above: Selling a Wife, 1814. A pen-and-ink sketch by Thomas Rowlandson (1756-1827) of the English custom of wife-selling.

the late-seventeenth century and is recorded as occurring as late as the opening of the twentieth century. A legalised divorce was an option only for the wealthy; it required a private Act of Parliament, i.e., an exception to the draconian British divorce law of the time, which was a costly and time-consuming process beyond the reach of most people. And so they turned to a custom that had no basis in law, but was regarded as a valid public faux-divorce. A couple looking to dissolve a marriage would partake in a public auction, in which the wife was publicly displayed, and her positive attributes listed. As grim as it sounds,

contemporary sources describe it as actually being beneficial to both parties; the winning 'bidder' was commonly the wife's lover, and all were then free to go on their merry way.

One of the most notable instances of wife-selling is mentioned in biographies of Henry Brydges, 2nd Duke of Chandos (1708-71). The duke first met his second wife, Anne Wells, when on his way to London he stopped to dine at the Pelican Inn in Newbury, where she worked as a chambermaid. Word went around that a man was selling his wife in the yard, and the duke went outside to see a woman being auctioned off by a foul husband. The duke paid for her freedom, and they were later married on Christmas Day in 1744, remaining together until her death in 1759.

The Unicorn Tapestries *(1495-1505)*

The myth of the elusive unicorn had been alive in the popular imagination for over 1,600 years by the time Sir Thomas Browne included it in his wonderful *Pseudodoxia Epidemica* of 1646, a volume in which he lances popular misconceptions and superstitions of his time. By then, with its widespread use in literature and art, the unicorn had come to symbolise everything from fertility and seduction, to purity, divinity, healing and sacrifice. So perhaps it is somewhat surprising that, when it comes to the magnificent set of seven giant weavings of fine wool, silver and gold known as The *Unicorn Tapestries, or The Hunt of the Unicorn*, in the collection of the Metropolitan Museum of Art in New York, there is still no consensus as to what the unicorn and the scenes represent, why they were made nor who commissioned them. We also have no clue as to the identity of the artist of this most beautiful of mysteries inherited from the Middle Ages, with their dyes of madder (red), woad (blue) and weld (yellow) still vibrant, nor which order they should be presented in.

The leading theory is that the tapestries are a set of cryptic ceremonial marriage documents, commissioned to celebrate the union of a wealthy couple by telling the story of a unicorn being hunted and caught. The story also seems to be an allegory of Christ's Passion, as there are symbols of this too. In the tapestry known as *The Hunters Enter the Woods*, the setting is a *millefleurs* background of a lush green field filled with all sorts of flowers and blossoming trees, including a cherry tree. (Some 101 species of plants are represented in the seven tapestries, of which eighty-five have been identified.) As our eyes adjust, we notice the cipher 'A & E' woven into the trunk of the cherry tree, and then again

Opposite: The Hunters Enter the Woods.   *Above:* The Unicorn in Captivity.

in another four different parts of the scene. These letters, it is assumed, allude to the original owners of the tapestries, but their identities remain a mystery. The spotter in the tree waves excitedly to the hunters: the unicorn has been sighted. In *The Unicorn is Found*, the beast is discovered before a fountain decorated with goldfinches and pheasants, dipping its horn into a stream to perhaps purify the water that pours from the fountain. Encircling this is a group of twelve hunters, the same number as Christ's disciples. Plants once used as medieval herbal antidotes to poisoning – sage, pot marigolds, orange – are dotted beside the stream.

In *The Unicorn is Attacked*, the scene is suddenly one of chaotic battle. Horns are

The Unicorn is Found.

blown as the hunters attempt to plunge their lances into the animal's flesh as it leaps across the stream to escape. (Again, the cipher 'A & E' can be found in the four corners and on the oak tree in the centre.) The injured creature fights back in *The Unicorn Defends Itself*, furiously kicking at a hunter while lacerating a greyhound nearly in two with its horn. The hunter blowing a horn in the lower-left corner carries a scabbard with the dangling inscription *ave regina c[oeli]* (Hail, Queen of the Heavens).

The Unicorn Captured by the Virgin exists in two small fragments, appearing to show

the unicorn trapped in a fenced garden and submitting to a maiden, who signals to a hunter to sound the horn. *The Unicorn is Killed and Brought to the Castle* contains two panels of story, and the clearest allegory to Christ's Passion. On the left we find the hunters stabbing the unicorn to death with their blades, with one of their number using a horn to catch the falling blood, reminiscent of depictions of the Crucifixion in which angels scoop Christ's blood in chalices. In the centre the unicorn is now slung across the back of a horse, its neck ringed with a crown of thorns like Christ, as it is presented to a group of royals.

And finally there is the most beloved of the tapestries, the main image shown at the beginning of this chapter, *The Unicorn in Captivity*, which might well have been created

The Unicorn is Attacked.

as a single piece and not as part of the series. The unicorn appears content in his captivity, loosely tied to a tree behind a fence he could easily leap over if he so wished. The tree bears ripe pomegranates, a medieval symbol of fertility and marriage, which has led to the hypothesis that this particular piece was made to be hung by the bed of a noble couple on their wedding night.

Solutions to the enigma of the tapestries have been confidently offered in the past. 'This puzzling quest is almost at its end,' wrote the first curator of the Met Cloisters (where they are displayed to this day), James Rorimer, in 1942, who had been handed the daunting task of their interpretation.

Above: The Unicorn Defends Itself.

Right: Fragments from The Unicorn Surrenders to a Maiden.

The museum was donated the works in 1937 by the American financier John D. Rockefeller Jr (1874-1960), who had acquired them from the La Rochefoucauld family in 1922. The French nobles had owned them since at least 1680, although the tapestries had briefly left their possession in the 1790s, when they were looted during the French Revolution. They were later found with tattered edges and holes, having been used to wrap fruit trees over winter. Rorimer claimed to have found symbols in the weavings – including a knotted

cord, a pair of striped tights and a squirrel – that he said revealed Anne of Brittany to have been their original owner, in celebration of her marriage to Louis XII in 1499.

In 1976 an assistant curator named Margaret Freeman published a book that overturned Rorimer's theories. While it was possible that they were made as part of a marriage celebration, the interpretation of the symbols didn't hold up. 'The squirrel of the tapestry may be intended to be symbolic,' she wrote, 'or it may be present merely to call attention to the tree in which it sits.' As Rorimer's theories were gradually edited out of the museum's official guides,

The Unicorn is Found.

the information agreed as fact by consensus shrank to the extent that, as the former Met Cloisters lecturer Danielle Oteri has pointed out, today the wall labels that hang beside one of the world's most famous and intriguing set of artworks consist of only about one sentence each. 'It is among the greatest visual poems that I know. It is alluring and elusive like the unicorn itself,' Thomas P. Campbell, former director and CEO of the Metropolitan Museum of Art, told the *Paris Review* in 2020. 'I have no doubt that people will be spinning stories and interpretation for generations to come.'

The Heart Through the Ages

In some ways, it seems strange that the most prevalent symbol of romance, the heart shape, is an image of an internal organ that actually bears little resemblance to the organ itself. So, where did this idea come from?

Since antiquity, of all the mysterious parts of the body the heart was always thought of as the core of being, drumming the rhythm of life. In his treatise *De anima* (On the Soul) written *c.*350 BC, Aristotle posits the home of the soul to be not the brain, as Plato suggests, but the heart. It was from this chambered residence that the soul governed all love and other emotions and actions. It was an ancient Greek theory in part influenced by examinations of chicken embryos, that suggested the heart was the first organ to develop: nature apparently gave preference to its most powerful component.

This was the ancient cardiovascular knowledge inherited and built on by later writers like the Greek physician Galen (129-*c.*216) and the Persian polymath Ibn

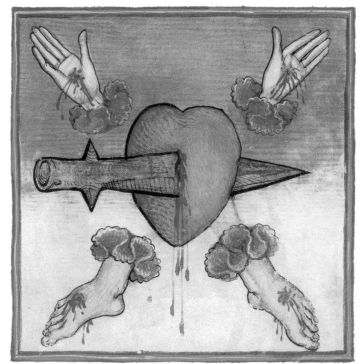

Top Right: Christ's stigmata wounds, from the Prayerbook of Georg II of Waldburg *(1486).*

Bottom Right: This is the earliest known image of the heart drawn as a symbol of romantic love, an illumination from a French medieval manuscript of the romance Le roman de la poire *(The Romance of the Pear) from the 1250s. Here, the male protagonist (an allegorical figure of* doux regard, *or 'sweet gaze') offers his heart, in the shape of a pear, to his lover. The pear is similar to the 'pine cone' shape with which Galen and Ibn Sina describe the heart.*

Sina (980-1036), who wrote of the heart as being the source of the body's healing ability and generator of its growth. Together with Aristotle and Plato, these authorities would dominate medieval understanding of the body for centuries. Surprisingly little study was made of the heart, which is partly why we find it illustrated in such varying forms in manuscripts. It wouldn't be until the seventeenth century, with the work of the English physician William Harvey (1578-1657), that its role in the systemic circulation of blood was completely described for the first time.

The emotional importance of the heart is celebrated in early linguistic terms still used today: 'courage' comes from the Old French *coeur* for heart; while 'core', as in our emotional centre, and 'record' (as, to learn something 'by heart'), both come from the same Latin root for heart, *cor*, or *cordis*. As the home of our emotions, the heart was attributed as the driving force of love from as early as the tenth century, when the Jewish Egyptian physician-poet Moses Ben Abraham Dar'I wrote of the heart offering greater guidance than the eyes:

To the one who asks me to reveal the name
of my beloved,
I cry out: 'You suffer from a blind heart!'
For when the light in one's eyes grows dim,
the eyes of the heart will always begin to see.

Giraut de Bornelh, writing in France in the 1180s, saw the eyes as hardworking servants of the heart:

So through the eyes love attains the heart.
For the eyes are the scouts of the heart,
And the eyes go searching
For what would please the heart to possess.

This identity of the heart then becomes a staple of tales of the courtly love genre, in which troubadours and minstrels sing of knights wooing noble ladies. Graphically,

however, the heart evolves as a symbol, undergoing surprising changes, as illustrated by the gallery of images on the next two pages.

Below: In Giotto's 1305 allegorical painting of Charity in the Scrovegni Chapel, Padua, we find charity presenting her heart to Jesus Christ. Again, the heart is depicted with a pine-cone shape in line with contemporary anatomical descriptions. Just like the previous image, the pine-cone heart is held upside-down, a style that switches in the late fourteenth century.

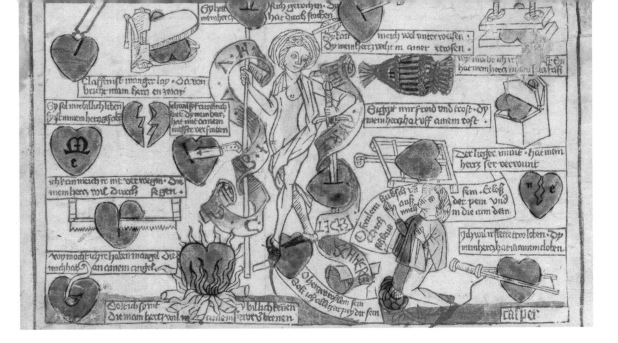

Below: In Young Man Holding a Book, *painted in Brussels c.1480, a reader clasps a cordiform manuscript similar to the one shown to the right.*

Above: In this 1485 print Frau Minne ('Lady Courtly Love'), a favourite figure of German artists, symbolises heartbreak by torturing nineteen hearts in various ways — burning, sawing, pressing — while a helpless lover looks on, aghast.

Right: At some point in the fifteenth century the heart-shape symbol ♥ *replaces the early medieval pine-cone shape, though it's not known how this change happened — perhaps, with the association of spring (see Valentine's Day on page 200) with new love, the lea-flike symbol became popular. Regardless, by the 1470s the* ♥ *symbol has come to represent the heart, which is why we find it as the shape of the extraordinary* Chansonnier Cordiforme (1470s), *otherwise known as the* Chansonnier de Jean de Montchenu, *a French cordiform (heart-shaped) music manuscript commissioned between 1460 and 1477 by Canon Jean de Montchenu. When opened it becomes two hearts joined, representing the two lovers who send love notes to each other in the songs.*

Left: In Japan, since ancient times the heart symbol like that shown on this seventeenth-century arrowhead is called inome *and used to ward off evil spirits. Meaning literally 'boar's eye', the heart-shaped element represents the ferociousness of a provoked wild boar, and can be found decorating Japanese armour and weapons, as well as Shinto shrines and Buddhist temples.*

Above: Augustine of Hippo holding a heart in his hand, set ablaze by a ray emanating from divine Truth (Veritas), in a painting by Philippe de Champaigne (1602-74), c.1650.

Right: The leaden funerary casket containing the heart of German Imperial Field Marshal Christoph Otto von Velen, who died in 1733, held in Raesfeld chapel, Germany.

Below: A printed 'Vinegar Valentine' from the late nineteenth century, when it was a tradition around Valentine's Day to send anonymous anti-romantic messages (see page 203 for another).

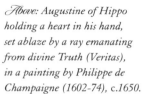

A WARNING
Pray take an honest friend's advice,
Or you will have to pay the price.
Your idle tongue must cease to wag,
Or it will wear this warning tag.

Above: Sacred Heart of Jesus with Saint Ignatius of Loyola and Saint Louis Gonzaga, c.1770, *by the Mexican painter José de Páez (c.1720-90).*

The Iron Spider
or, Adultery: A Cheat Sheet

A remarkable characteristic of human nature is our irrepressible curiosity in the forbidden – the more something is prohibited, the more we want to learn about it/do it/eat it. One area in which we find this exemplified is how the strictness of adultery laws is matched by its popularity as a theme in contemporary literature.

These laws are found in the earliest rule books: the Code of Hammurabi of eighteenth-century BC Babylonia instructs execution by drowning for adultery; while in ancient Greek and Roman law capital punishment could also be prescribed for the female spouse but men more usually got off lightly. Before the unification of England in the tenth century, there were a variety of laws codified by Anglo-Saxon kings covering adultery. In the seventh century, for example, the Law of Æthelberht, king of Kent, allowed for men to apply for compensation or seek revenge in the event that other men had sex with their women. This stipulated that not only should a financial amount be provided, but also a replacement wife: 'if a free-man lies with [another] free-man's wife, he shall pay [the husband] his wergeld [a fine] and procure a second wife with his own money and bring her to the other man's home'. The ninth-century Laws of Alfred of Wessex permitted the aggrieved husband to attack the adulterous male 'if he finds another with his wedded wife, behind closed doors or under the same blanket'. This principle continued until the Laws of Henry I of 1114-18, which decreed that only the king had the authority to punish the male adulterer, and the bishops the power to punish the female adulterer.

Jules Arsène Garnier's (1847-89) The Adulterers' Punishment *(1876).*

Meanwhile, we have adultery as a popular running theme through the history of literature. We can find it in Chapter 16 of the Book of Genesis in the Old Testament, when Abram sleeps with his wife's Egyptian slave Hagar in order to procreate; or the numerous Greek myths involving Zeus sleeping with a long list of goddesses and mortals, sometimes by turning himself into animals, to the despair of his sister-wife Hera. In fact, as a story-telling device adultery propels much of Europe's most beloved literature in the Middle Ages, from romance to fabliaux. *The Tale of the Châtelain de Coucilet and the Lady of Fayel*, for example, written at the end of the thirteenth century by a 'Jakemon Sakesep', tells the story of Raoul de Couci, who leaves for battle with a jewelled box containing braids of hair of his married lover, La Dame de Fayel, which she gave him as a sign of her devotion. De Couci is struck by a poisoned arrow during the fight, and as he lies dying he orders his servant to cut out his heart, store it in the jewelled box and present it to his lover with a letter declaring that his heart belongs to her. Unfortunately, the lady's husband intercepts the package, discovers the heart, and secretly has it cooked into a meal for his wife. When La Dame de Fayel realises that she has eaten her lover's heart, she refuses to eat again, and dies soon after.

Dante devotes the entire second circle of Hell in his *Inferno* to the adulterous damned, where during his visit he encounters the real-life figure of Francesca da Rimini (1255-*c*.1285), who was murdered by her husband, Giovanni Malatesta, upon his discovery of Francesca's affair with his brother, Paolo Malatesta. Francesca is the first soul of Hell in the work to have a substantial speaking role, as she testifies to her story, in what is the first historical record of her. In their circle of Hell

While visiting the second circle of Hell for the lustful, Dante encounters the adulterous Francesca da Rimini (1255-c.1285), who was murdered by her husband, Giovanni Malatesta, upon his discovery of Francesca's affair with his brother, Paolo Malatesta.

Francesca and her lover Paolo are rocked by violent winds, like the passions that swept them away. Paolo weeps in the background while Francesca tells Dante her story, blaming their situation on being helpless victims of love: 'Love, which is swiftly kindled in the noble heart, seized this one for the lovely person that was taken from me; and the manner still injures me … Love led us on to one death.'

Usually with adulterous tales of this era a moral code was observed and the lovers were eventually caught – but not always. Take for example two stories from the *Gesta Romanorum*, a popular collection of tales compiled at around the end of the thirteenth century, which demonstrate the medieval fondness for smart characters outwitting the gullible to get away with their crimes.

In the first, as a knight leaves home to collect grapes from his vineyard his wife calls for her lover and they head straight for the bedroom. Unfortunately, the husband injures his eye and heads home early. The wife quickly hides her lover before her husband enters, who, groaning from the pain, lies down on the bed. His wife convinces him that she should take care of the good eye, to prevent the injury spreading to it. And so she blindfolds him with a giant bandage, and her lover escapes. (The moral of the story, as the author sees it, is that the gullible husband is like the prelates of the Church: 'The prelate's eye is struck out as often as it is blinded by gifts.')

In the second story the husband is a soldier who leaves his elderly mother in the care of his wife. The wife takes a lover, but one night the husband returns unexpectedly, exhausted from battle. While the lover has been stashed from sight, the husband asks that his bed be prepared so that he can rest. The wife panics, but the mother saves the day by saying, 'Before you go, my child, let us show your husband the fair sheet which we have made.' The women then dangle a cloth in front of his face, while the lover takes the cue to escape behind it unseen. 'The wife is the flesh; the mother is the world; and the sheet, worldly vanities,' explains the author, trying to give substance to his soap opera.

A more famous example is 'The Miller's Tale' from Geoffrey Chaucer's *Canterbury Tales* (1380s-1390s), in which Alisoun cheats on her husband John with their young lodger

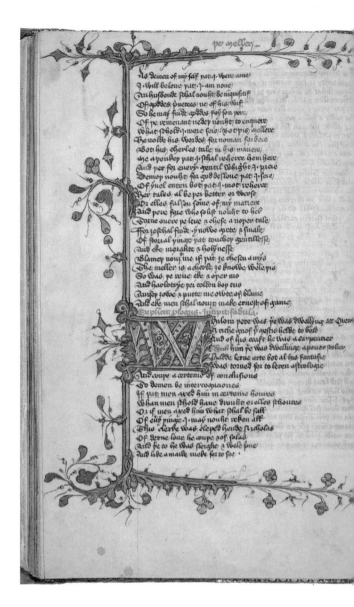

Made c.1410, about a decade after Chaucer's death, this manuscript is the earliest known copy of his Canterbury Tales. *'The Miller's Tale' begins on this page with the historiated initial.*

Nicholas, while also fending off the advances of another young man, Absolon, by offering her backside when the latter comes calling for a kiss. Enraged at having been tricked into kissing her 'ers' in the dark, he grabs a red-hot coulter (part of a plough) and returns to ask

Alisoun for another kiss. Unfortunately, this time it is Nicholas who sticks his backside out of the window to relieve himself and receives some karmic comeuppance for his adultery.

All of which farcical storytelling could give the impression of adultery as being taken lightly, which was anything but the case. The most extreme example of its ecumenical classification as a crime just short of murder is the torture instrument graphically known as the Breast Ripper (a fifteenth-century German example is shown here), and a similar device known as the 'Iron Spider'. Misogyny dominates the history of torture, but this device is especially shocking, heated up and used to punish women condemned for adultery, pregnancy out of wedlock, self-performed abortions and 'erotic white magic'.

In England it wasn't until 1857, with the passing of the Matrimonial Causes Act, that the jurisdiction over marriage, divorce and adultery was transferred from the ecclesiastical courts to the civil courts. Prior to this act passing, nineteenth-century ecclesiastical punishments for adultery usually involved some form of public penance, like appearing before the parish congregation in a penitential white sheet. Even then, the act did not treat the grounds for divorce for men and women equally. Men could be granted divorce if their wife committed adultery, but a wife would only be granted a divorce if her husband had also committed other offences as well. Only with the Matrimonial Causes Act of 1923 was this imbalance corrected.

Even in the modern era, legal considerations of adultery can vary. For example, in America, adultery in Washington State has no bearing on a divorce as either party can apply for one without needing to provide proof of a cause. In New York, however, adultery remains a crime, as it does

A fifteenth-century example of the medieval torture device known as the Breast Ripper, applied as punishment to adulterous women. From the collection of the torture museum in Freiburg im Breisgau, Baden-Württemberg, Germany.

in North Carolina, which is one of the few states that also allows for the aggrieved spouse to sue the third party and request the judge and jury to order punitive compensatory damages be paid. With same-sex relationships, there was a little catching-up to do in the way of legislative definition: in the 2003 New Hampshire Supreme Court case Blanchflower v. Blanchflower, it was held that female same-sex sexual relations did not constitute sexual intercourse as based on a 1961 definition from *Webster's Third New International Dictionary*. Therefore, an accused wife in a divorce case was found not guilty of adultery.

The Tower of Jealousy – Love in Medieval Manuscripts

For the medieval literate who sought courting advice, romantic tales, medicinal cures for a broken heart, or even just titillation, answers could be found in the manuscripts hand-copied and illuminated by monks toiling away in scriptoriums. The sources were wildly varied, from classical romances of historical and mythological characters, like the adventures of King Arthur or the many reimagined origin stories of Alexander the Great, to the inherited knowledge of authorities of antiquity like the wobbly scientific theories of Galen and the love tips of Ovid. While these names are most likely familiar to today's reader, with the subject of love being of such universal interest a number of other curious and less well-known manuscripts were produced that are also a delight to explore.

The Romance of the Rose, for instance, is a colossal poem of Old French presented as an allegorical dream vision, that purports to cover the entire art of chivalric romance as a 'mirror of love'. Begun *c.*1230 by Guillaume de Lorris, who wrote 4,058 verses, the story follows the

Lover's request for the Rose, a symbol of his lady's love. He discovers a walled garden belonging to the noble Déduit (the Old French word for pleasure), and under the tutorship of the winged God of Love sets about trying to find the Rose. Forty-five years later in *c.*1275 the work was completed by the French author Jean de Meun with an additional 17,724 lines, taking the story beyond the garden's walls, and realising de Lorris's vision of a comprehensive philosophical discussion of love. One of the most widely read books of the fourteenth and fifteenth centuries (around three hundred manuscript copies survive), it infuriated moralists with its sensual language and illustrations, and yet escaped unpunished by the Church.

Opposite: The Tower of Jealousy, guarded by a garrison of soldiers and the bearded figure of Danger grasping the keys in the lower-centre section. From an illuminated manuscript copy of the Romance of the Rose *made c.1490-1500.*

Left: Another allegorical teaching, with the use of the popular light-hearted theme of the Castle of Love (see another example on page 79) under siege from romantic knights, with maidens deploying flowers as a defence. From the Luttrell Psalter, 1325-40.

A mtenant est
sont quelodie
La contenance
sa ialousie
Q ui est male suspection
Il ny eust on pays macon
ne prommier quelle ne mande
Si leur fait faire et command
Entre les rosiers du fosse
Q ui cousteront demar asses

Car ils sont sarcies et pafone
Dessue les bors sont les macons
Ung mur dequarreaux bie taillie
Bien appointez et habillez
Dont le fondement par mesme
Est assis sur roche tresdure
Iusque au pie du fosse descent
Et vient amont en estrissent
Loeuure en est plus forte defsa
Les murs furent si compasse

Above: An engraving by Albrecht Dürer (1471-1528) for the 1493 German translation of The Book of the Knight of the Tower.

Below: An illustration of the German poet Konrad von Altstetten (fl.1320) embracing his lover, from the Codex Manesse, which carries 135 miniature portraits of different poets.

Every aspect of love is covered, including warnings of the gloomier side of courting, dealing with emotions of anger, melancholy and jealousy. The illustration shown on page 123 is one of ninety-two illustrations from the exceptional *c.*1500 copy in the collection of the British Library. Here, 'The Tower of Jealousy Where Fair Welcome is Imprisoned' is shown in a detailed miniature, where the Rose is held captive. The lover lingers outside the walls, unable to pass the figure of Dangier (Danger), who holds the keys to the gate, and the garrison of soldiers who guard the Rose in the tower.

With the advent of Johannes Gutenberg's movable type printing press in around 1440 came the ability to mass-produce texts and circulate them widely, and *The Romance of the Rose* and a few other of these love-themed manuscripts would prove to be the equivalent of bestsellers. One is known in English as *The Book of the Knight of the Tower*, which was begun in 1371 by the French nobleman Sir Geoffroy IV de la Tour Landry. The widowed knight's intention was to create a book of advice for his young daughters on the etiquette involved in visiting court, the dangers of vanity, and most importantly, the tricks and pitfalls in dealing with slick young courtiers looking to take advantage of naive maidens. 'I saw my daughters coming towards me,' he begins. 'I wanted to make them a little book to read so they might learn and study and understand the good and evil that has already happened, in order to keep them from that which is yet to come.'

It remains a fascinating book, providing insight into the social expectations of women and the entirely relatable concerns of a medieval parent sending his daughters out into a dangerous world. The advice from a man who had fought and survived battles of the Hundred Years War gives a tough and realistic sense of the era – a wife must put up with her husband's harshness, and be absolutely obedient, for example. Many of the lessons are taught through stories, like the importance of remaining devout and not giving away one's body. Sir Geoffroy writes of two young and unworldly Byzantine princesses, one pious, the other sinful. They fell in love with two different knights, who came at night to visit them. The prospective lover of the pious princess was suddenly hit with a vision of her surrounded by a thousand religious men in shrouds, which made him flee in terror. The second lover spent the night with the sinful princess with no problem and she became pregnant. When the girls' father, the emperor, discovered this, he drowned the sinful princess and had the lover flayed alive. The pious princess went on to marry a great king and was loved by all.

The book was popular for centuries. William Caxton translated it into English in 1483, and in 1493 came a German translation, *Der Ritter vom Turm*, by a Swabian noble named Marquard von Stain, who claimed to have been motivated to do so for his own two daughters Elsa and Jakobea.

Alternatively, for young men seeking help in making a success of their love life, there is the manuscript known as the Codex Manesse of *c*.1304, a Middle High German *Liederhandschrift* (manuscript song collection) renowned as one of the most beautiful German manuscripts ever produced. The book collects the love poetry of 135 different poets, with each work accompanied by a portrait of the poet. Rather than using any chronological or alphabetical ordering system, the book presents the poets in order of social status, opening with Holy Roman Emperor Henry VI, and working its way through dukes and knights to commoners.

Some young men in possession of the requisite skills went a step further and produced their own illuminated manuscript for the target of their affections (a tradition

Illustration from Pierre Sala's Petit Livre d'Amour *(*Little Book of Love*), c.1500.*

upheld by Henry Hilditch Bulkeley-Johnson of page 212). One of the most renowned of these custom romantic gifts is the adorable *Petit Livre d'Amour* (Little Book of Love), *c*.1500, of the French writer Pierre Sala (*c*.1457-*c*.1529). Though he was writing at a time when printing was in full swing, Sala preferred the art of the illuminated manuscript, producing single copies of books of verse, fables and emblems. He created his *Little Book of Love* for Marguerite Bullioud – the capital letter 'M' along with his initial 'P' appear in the quatrains written in gold cursive, as well as carved into the decorative adornments in the images. The last of the full-page miniatures in the book is a portrait of himself, painted by his friend, the skilled miniaturist Jean Perréal. The book must have done the trick; Sala successfully wooed Bullioud, and the two were later married.

Within the illustration:

ſlous monſtre tres dous dier me
telgnant laigreſe.
Quant uoulistes pour nous
couſtur tant de distreſce.

Opposite: Sex and nudity have always been popular instruments of storytelling device, even (or especially) with the scribes and artists who spent their lives copying medieval manuscripts. Here, in this tempera-and-gold illumination, Bathsheba, temptress of King David, is shown bathing while he sneaks a peek. In contrast to the biblical account, Bathsheba gives a complicit look back. From the Hours of Louis XII (1498-9), one of the greatest French manuscripts of its time.

Above: The wound of Christ, from the Prayer Book of Bonne of Luxembourg, Duchess of Normandy before 1349, attributed to Jean Le Noir of France. In the later Middle Ages, devotion became intensely focused on the wounds of the bodily torment of Christ, and images such as this in private manuscripts, in which the wound is an entrance to and exit from the body, continue to be discussed for their compelling similarity to a vagina, perhaps from which the Church was born.

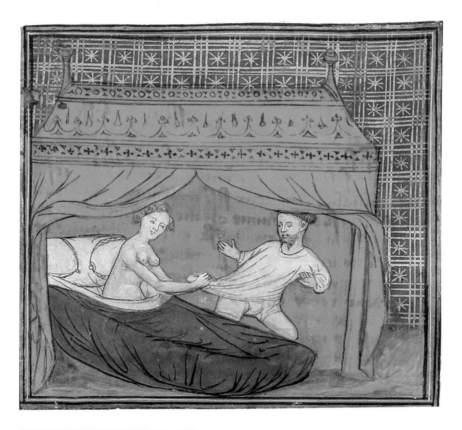

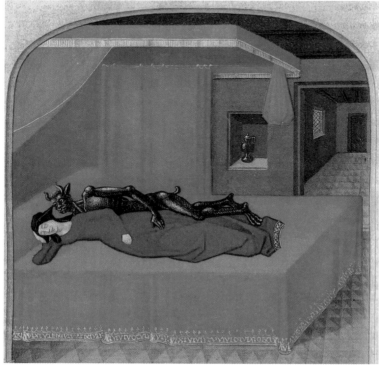

Top Left: Princess Elaine of Corbenic, daughter of the Fisher King, seduces Lancelot by magically tricking him into thinking that she's Guinevere. From a copy of Le livre de Lancelot du Lac, *c.1401-25.*

Bottom Left: According to Arthurian tradition, Merlin was 'demon born'. This illustration from Histoire de Merlin *(c.1450-5) shows a demon visiting Merlin's mother in the night.*

Opposite: How Alexander was conceived: Olympias, his mother, is shown naked in bed with a dragon, which is actually Nectanebus, the magician-astrologer king of Egypt, in disguise. Olympias's husband Philip spies on them through an opening. From a French manuscript copy of Book of the Works of Alexander the Great, *c.1468-75, one of many whimsical 'Alexander romances'.*

Magical Papyrus 121; and the Love Spell

'Take a shell from the sea and draw on it with myrrh ink the figure of Typhon [a demon] given below,' instructs the author of this ancient love spell to win the heart of an indifferent man, from a magical Greek papyrus of fourth-century Egypt in the collection of the British Library. 'In a circle write his names and throw it into the heating of a hot bath. But when you throw it, keep reciting these words: "Attract to me X, whom X bore, on this very day from this very hour, with a soul and a heart aflame, quickly, quickly; immediately, immediately."'

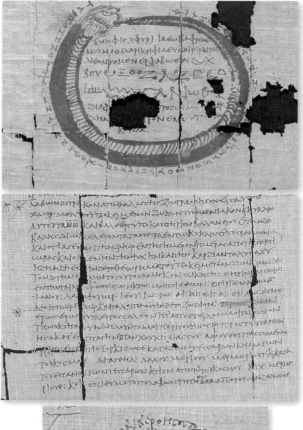

In the same papyrus there are instructions for those looking for a spell of more direct action, with a special invocation to Selene, goddess of the Moon, here referred to as 'mistress of the entire world'. Mix together clay, sulphur and the blood of a dappled goat to mould a statue of the goddess, and consecrate an olive wood shrine that is turned to never face the Sun. In return, Selene will dispatch a holy angel to physically drag the terrified and sleepless object (victim?) of affection to the caster of the spell. Success was guaranteed, for 'the power of the spell is strong'.

Whether it's early Greek papyrus spell rolls like this example, or the ancient Mesopotamian cuneiform tablets dug up at Tell Inghara and Isin (present-day Iraq) dating to 2200 BC, or the notorious grimoires of Early Modern Europe, magical manuscripts were commonly composed of spells of two main categories of interest. The first was treasure-hunting. Traditional belief held that buried treasure was guarded by ghosts and demons, and therefore to learn the location of the loot and secure its release, magic instructions were needed to conjure and

Opposite: Circe Offering the Cup to Ulysses *(1891), John William Waterhouse (1849-1917). The seductive enchantress Circe offers a cup with a magical potion to Odysseus to bring him under her spell. However, having been warned by Hermes of this ahead of time, Odysseus has ingested the herb Moly and remains immune to her charms.*

control the spirits that kept it. In 1466, for example, a Robert Barker of Cambridgeshire was charged by his bishop with possessing a book and charts of strange figures, and a gilded wand designed to summon spirits and find hidden gold. He was sentenced to trudge barefoot around Cambridge market while his magical equipment was burned in the square. In 1429 in Poland, a member of the royal household named Henry the Bohemian confessed to conjuring up treasure with two professors of Krakow University in the royal zoological garden. (Not exactly the most inconspicuous choice of location for a tremendously illegal activity, one would think, but such is the passion of the treasure-hunting hobbyist sorcerer.)

The second most common type of spell was love magic. A confession from 1517 of a priest of Modena named Don Campana is documented in which he admits that 'he once had a book, called *Clavicula Salomonis*, and another book called *Almandel*, and some other booklets and writings with many love magic instructions, and he said he burned them all.' While some love charms were mild restoratives for the heartbroken, others promised to enhance the sexual experience and solidify the longevity of a relationship, while darker forms of binding magic offered the power to captivate and satanically seduce an intended target. In 1410 in Carcassonne, south-western France, a notary named Geraud Cassendi was found by an inquisitor to have tried to debauch local women through invoking demons using a grimoire and scrapings of gold taken from an image of the Virgin. Also in Carcassonne, a monk named Pierre Recordi was imprisoned for life for the same crime, having confessed (under torture) to offering to the Devil wax puppets filled with his saliva and the blood of toads.

Love magic could also be weaponised against rivals, by robbing them of their sexual appetite and ability. In the grimoire known as *The Picatrix*, for example, we find the following instructions for magically induced impotence:

When you wish to bind a man or woman, make an image of a man whose feet are raised to the heavens and whose head is in the ground. This should be made of wax, saying 'I have bound N. son of such-and-such a woman, and all his veins, until he does not have a man's desire.' After that, bury the image in his path, and he will not use a woman for as long as the image lasts. And it is said by some that this image is made under the second decan of Aries.

With spells such as this compounding their diabolical reputation, it is perhaps little wonder why such volumes were so enthusiastically hurled onto bonfires – and why their authors were sometimes hurled along with them.

Following Pages:
Left: A page from a Hebrew version of the Picatrix *of c.1500-99, a magician's grimoire that details both gentle and sinister forms of love magic.*

Right: Der Neid (Envy), a warning against the use of sorcerer spells to obtain, among other things, the love of another's spouse. From the magical manuscript known as A Most Rare Compendium of the Whole Magical Art *(after 1792) in the collection of the Wellcome Library, London.*

Opposite: Liebeszauber (The Love Spell) 1470-80, unidentified artist.

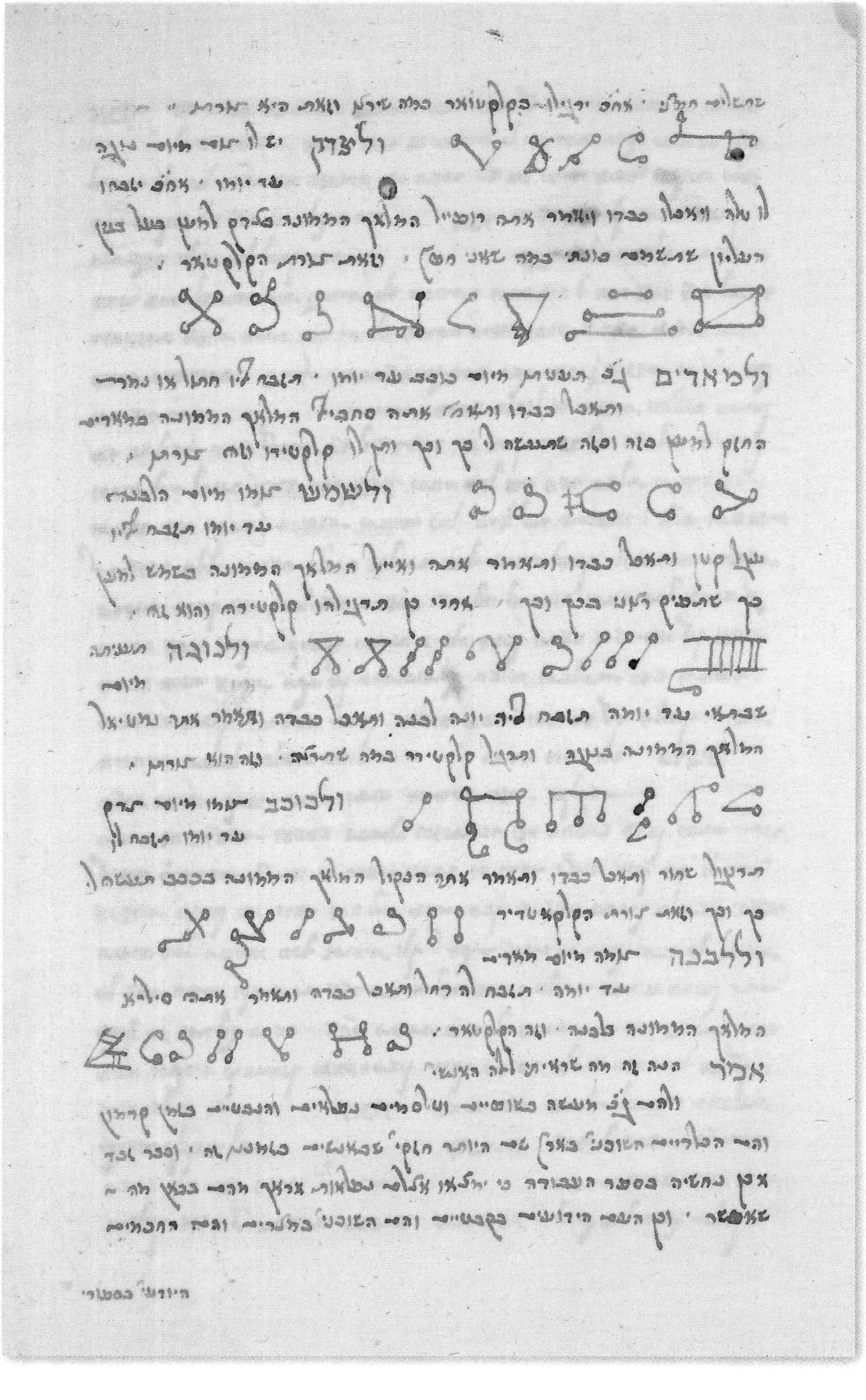

Der Neid.

Unlocking the Chastity Belt

The chastity belt is one of those strange historical objects that has an inverse lifespan, becoming less legendary and more real as time goes on. Certainly, today it exists not just in widespread popular imagination but also the bedside tables of BDSM practitioners, and even, occasionally, newspaper headlines. On 6 February 2004, for example, *USA Today* reported that a metal detector at Athens airport in Greece had been set off by a female holidaymaker wearing a steel chastity belt. She was allowed to continue on her flight to London after explaining her husband had forced her to wear it on her vacation to prevent any extramarital affairs. And the *China People's Daily* reported on 12 September 2012 of a gentleman in his fifties named Liu who appeared naked but for a homemade chastity belt in Changchun World Sculpture Park in north-eastern Jilin Province, China, holding aloft banners announcing his desire for a wife from the region. 'I want to broadcast my willingness to marry as quickly as possible,' he said, claiming that the chastity belt showed his commitment to fidelity. 'I don't think he'll find a wife this way,' said an onlooker.

Popular legend dictates that the contraption known as the chastity belt, designed to obstruct any sexual intercourse (either wanted or unwanted), dates all the way back to the Crusades of the eleventh-thirteenth centuries, when knights would literally lock up the virtue of their spouses while they were away at battle or on pilgrimage. What has always puzzled historians about this cornerstone of medieval lore, however, is the lack of surviving specimens and the (almost total) lack of contemporary mention of the concept of it in texts. Could they in fact be Victorian myth? The example shown here, for instance, which would have been lined with velvet, is held in the collection of the Wellcome Library, London, and though it was acquired with accompanying documentation dating it to the 1500s, the institution notes that it was likely made in the 1800s.

One of the earliest references to the general concept was written in the second half of the twelfth century, when Marie de France (*fl.*1180) relates in the Guigemar Epic poem of the Breton knight Guigemar begging for a pledge of fidelity from his lady before he departs. She ties his shirt with a knot in such a way that only she can undo it without force. In turn, Guigemar ties a knotted girdle around her naked body, and she swears to only love him who is able to open it without any force.

This is not, though, the chastity belt as we – or indeed Mr Liu – would recognise it. For that we are pointed to the *Bellifortis*, an illustrated military encyclopedia of 1405 by Konrad Kyeser von Eichstadt in the collection of the University of Göttingen. Among the illustrations of war machines we find a very cumbersome-looking chastity belt, with a Latin annotation informing us that 'These are hard iron breeches of Florentine women which are closed at the front.' Writing later in the early seventeenth century, the French historian Pierre de Bourdeille, Abbé de Brantôme, wrote in his anecdotes of the occasion 'in the

Opposite: A chastity belt in the collection of the Wellcome Library, London, supposedly dating to the 1500s.

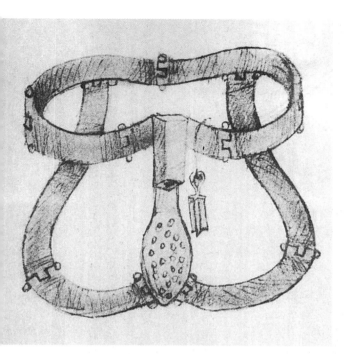

deep suspicion – certainly it is thought that none dates to before the sixteenth century, and that surviving specimens probably date to the nineteenth century. Two have been exhibited at the Musée de Cluny in Paris: one, fashioned out of velvet and iron, was said to have been worn by Catherine de' Medici (1519-89); while the other featured engraved illustrations of Adam and Eve and was said to have guarded the loins of Anne of Austria. In 1889, an example made of leather and iron was found in Linz, Austria, by an antiquities collector investigating the grave of a young woman supposedly buried in the sixteenth century. There was, however, no record of her interment in the town archives, and the belt has since been lost. Others can be found in the Germanisches Nationalmuseum in Nuremberg and the British Museum in London, but with their dubious authenticity are unlikely to be seen on display. If there is more to the story of the chastity belt and its true origins, it seems its secrets have yet to be unlocked.[1]

time of King Henry' when a metal-goods dealer brought several chastity belts operated by lock and key to sell at the fair at Saint-Germain: 'It was not possible that the woman, being restrained once, could ever avail herself of it for this sweet pleasure, having only a few tiny little holes to serve for pissing'. Several husbands bought the belts and bribed their wives to wear them. The problem, de Bourdeille relates, was that the women sought the help of a locksmith, who forged keys for the women to unlock them at will, so they could have sex with – yes, you guessed it – the locksmith. The metals dealer was threatened with death if he ever returned and attempted to sell the items again. He was also ordered to 'throw away all the others [down the drain] which he did; and since then it has not been spoken of.'

Examples of chastity belts can be found in museum collections, but are generally held in

---

1 The secrecy doesn't prevent modern inventors from adapting the idea, however. Take the Japanese firm Ravijour, which in 2014 released a bra that could only be unhooked when the wearer was in the presence of someone she loved. Advertised as 'the revolutionary bra that knows how women truly feel', the bra measures its wearer's heart rate to ascertain how 'in love', or aroused, she is, which the wearer can confirm with an app that sends a signal to the bra to unhook itself. (What isn't explained is what happens if the woman wants to take off the bra when alone.)

Legend of the Sex Nuts, and Other Stories of Love at Sea

The largest seed in the plant kingdom is that of the *Lodoicea* tree, commonly known as the sea coconut, coco de mer, or double coconut. Weighing in on average at 15-30kg, its size is certainly remarkable but its shape even more so, as it bears a striking resemblance to the disembodied buttocks of a woman on the front, and a woman's belly and thighs on the reverse. Hence its botanical name *Lodoicea callipyge*, from the Greek meaning 'beautiful buttocks'. For centuries it was the subject of fascination and legendary speculation. The rare species of palm tree can be found in the Seychelles archipelago in the Indian Ocean, from where the giant nuts occasionally drift via ocean current to other distant shores like those of the Maldives.

Before its origins were discovered, wild theories were put forward as to its seemingly magical nature. Malay sailors had witnessed the coco de mer nuts adrift in the ocean, apparently having 'fallen upwards' from the ocean floor, and so it was reasoned that the seeds grew on trees in a submerged forest beneath the water, on the bed of the Indian Ocean. Antonio Pigafetta (who would take command of Magellan's great circumnavigation after the explorer's violent death mid-journey) reported that the Malay people believed these trees to be the home of an enormous birdlike monster called the Garuda, which had a fondness for snatching elephants, and on occasion sailors trapped by waves caused by the subaquatic coco de mer trees.

After the discovery of the Seychelles, it was duly observed that only the female coco de mer trees carried the enormous seeds, while the male trees grew strikingly phallic catkins. And so local legend sprang up that on stormy nights the male trees would tear themselves from the ground, strut towards the females and have wild physical sex, producing more of their erotically shaped fruit. The fact that no one had ever actually *witnessed* this arbori-coitus was explained by the fact that the trees were shy and had the power to steal the sight of any human voyeur. (Even today the pollination of the coco de mer is not fully understood, so who knows.)

The legend of the sex nuts continued into the Victorian era, when a respected British Army officer and Christian cosmologist,

FERDINANDES MAGALANES LVSITANVS *anfractuoso euripo superato,* ⊗ *telluri ad Austrum nomen dedit,*
eiusque navis omnium prima, atque novissima Solis cursum in terris emulata, terræ totius globum circumijt. An. Sal. ∞·D·XXII.   4·

Major General Charles George Gordon,
declared the Seychelles to be the original
location of the Biblical Garden of Eden, and
the coco de mer nuts the forbidden fruit that
Adam had bitten into and handed to Eve. How
this would have been physically possible, given
the nuts' size, weight, and rock-hard exterior,
was not a question that anyone put to Gordon.

Meanwhile, in colder and decidedly less
erotic environs, whalers of the early nineteenth
century were developing a hobby-art that was
first referred to as 'scrimshaw' in a logbook
of 1826, although the origin of this name is
unknown. This is a style of scrollwork and
engraving in which (often crude) portraits of
spouses and family left behind, as well as naval

The mythical Garuda bird snatches an elephant in
the upper-left corner of this c.1592 engraving by
Stradanus, as the navigator Magellan sits on his ship
surrounded by all manner of creatures thought to haunt
the world's waters.

scenes and the remembered landscapes of
home, were carved into bone and teeth, usually
of whales, sometimes of walruses and, as a
last resort, cows. After carving with a needle,
soot or tobacco juice was then rubbed into the
lines to boost definition. The earliest surviving
scrimshaw is a tooth with an inscription that
reads: 'This is the tooth of a sperm whale that
was caught near the Galápagos Islands by the
crew of the ship Adam [of London] and made
100 barrels of oil in the year 1817.' Whaling

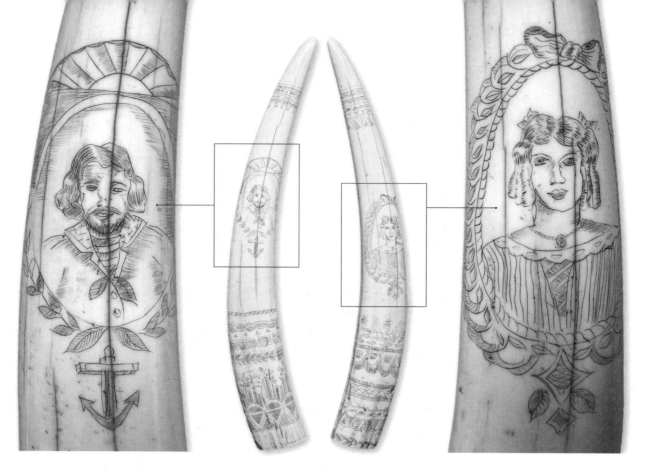

A pair of walrus tusks engraved c.1900 at Rhode Island or Connecticut with sailors' scrimshaw work.

was only conducted during the daytime, and so scrimshaw provided a way to while away the long evenings and create love tokens to gift upon one's return.

For a different class of traveller of the late eighteenth and nineteenth centuries, theirs was a voyage of no return home to loved ones. The National Museum of Australia has a large collection of what are known as 'convict coins', love tokens created by convicted felons given a sentence of transportation to the Australian colonies, for crimes for which capital punishment was deemed too severe. A custom developed in which such convicts would polish coins to a plain surface, and then etch their own messages and illustrations to give as mementos to their loved ones. Examples include a 1781 token (shown opposite top left) engraved by a Charles Croughton which reads: 'Charles Croughton, Birmingham, Wa[rw]ickshire 1781',

on one side, and on the reverse 'When this you sees / Remember me / tho' many leagu[e]s / we distant be= / March 4 / 1781'.

Another (opposite top right) dates from 1802 and features an elaborate border of leaves around an image of a woman leaning on a box, perhaps a coffin, with two hearts atop it, while pointing at a bird in the sky. The border features the words 'I love till death shall stop my breath'. They are extraordinarily poignant objects, small and crudely simple, yet sorrowful memorials of their creator and the love that has been torn apart. In many cases, these are the only surviving records, other than their prison ship manifests, of persons banished to the other side of the world for often minor transgressions.

Above Left: A coin engraved by a convict named Charles Croughton in 1781.

Above Right: An 1802 convict token with the inscription 'I love till death shall stop my breath.'

Below Left and Right: A convict coin dated 1826, etched by James Daws, a twenty-year-old African-English 'shopboy' convicted of stealing pennies, for which he was sentenced to seven years' transportation. He received a Certificate of Freedom in 1832.

Above: In 1825 a nineteen-year-old called Cornelius Donovan carved this 'cartwheel' penny while languishing on a prison hulk on the River Thames, waiting to begin his seven-year transportation sentence having stolen sewing cotton from a London shop. 'This is a token from my hand for I am going to Van Diemans Land', he writes, while on the reverse two lovebirds hover above a heart drawn around the paired initials 'EWN / CD'. The name of the recipient is unknown, as is the fate of Donovan after he landed in Van Diemen's land on 8 September 1825.

Below: Joseph Smyth was sentenced to death for burglary in 1817, but his sentence was commuted to transportation for life. He made this for his beloved wife Mary as a keepsake for her to remember him by. 'Joseph smyth / cast for death / 4th July 1817 / aged 33'. On the other side: 'Mary Ann Smyth / Aged 27'. In June 1819 Mary was convicted of pickpocketing, and also sentenced to transportation 'for life'. It's not known if they ever saw each other again.

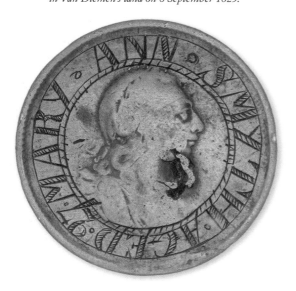

One of the conch shells collected by the famously severe Captain William Bligh, who was the subject of a mutiny on board his ship the Bounty by a disaffected crew led by Fletcher Christian. Bligh would collect shells on his travels around the South Seas, bringing them home as gifts for his wife Elizabeth, who formed one of the world's greatest collections. After her death the London dealer John Mauwe studied her collection to publish in 1821 'The Voyager's Companion or Shell Collectors Pilot', the world's first shell-collecting guide.

The Men Consumed by Flames (1600-10)

A man is engulfed in fire, and yet like the legendary salamander of antiquity he is untouched by the flames that dance around his head and across the arctic blue of his mantle. His cool expression and the absence of a single singed hair suggest him to be wholly unfazed by his situation. Around his head curl the words *Alget, qui non ardet:* 'He grows cold, who does not burn.' But who is this perpetually burning man, and how did he find himself in this predicament?

Isaac Oliver's highly detailed miniature portrait, seen here, which in its frame measures just 5.2 × 4.4cm (2 × 1¾ in), is perhaps the most intriguing example of the English Renaissance art of miniature portraiture. The tradition emerged from the techniques of manuscript illustrators, who would fashion complicated initials and vignettes of just a few centimetres in size on the page. In fact, the word 'miniature' comes from the Latin word *miniare*, which means 'to colour with red lead', a practice of manuscript scribes. In the minds of wealthy patrons, these small images would look even better as a luxury accessory worn around their necks or carried in pockets as mementos and devotional objects or given as tokens of love and admiration to family, friends or lovers.

With Oliver's *A Man Consumed by Flames* (*c.*1600-10), there is no record as to the identity of the subject, nor recorded explanation for the flame motif, but there are clues to be read. The subject is posed like the bust of a classical hero, the flames bouncing off his cool statue-like skin (a rigidity broken by the hint of a smile), in a state of relative undress. His gaze travels to connect with the intended recipient, an intimacy into which we are intruding from across the centuries. The traditional interpretation, given

Man Among Flames (c.1600), Nicholas Hilliard. Thought to have been painted a few years earlier than Oliver's work, again the identity of the subject is unknown. The young man chivalrously turns the picture box hanging around his neck towards his heart to hide the image of the object of his devotion. The goal of the miniaturist, wrote Hilliard, was to capture 'those lovely graces, witty smilings and those stolen glances which suddenly like lightning pass'.

the nature of miniatures serving as love tokens, is that this is a man caught in the flames of passion, perhaps caught in the suffering of unrequited love. The Latin motto could imply a burning love that only death can extinguish. It's a theme popular in Renaissance literature, but rare in this art – the only other known example is an earlier work by Oliver's mentor, Hilliard.

Miniaturists were only too happy to oblige with the demand for such tokens, having competed with the printed book since around 1460. Creating such objects was a demanding, and expensive, task. Possessing a steady hand was vital, as the artist had only two or three sittings to capture a likeness on a scrap of vellum about the size of a playing card. In fact, playing cards were often used to support the

painting: a miniature portrait of Elizabeth I in the collection of the National Portrait Gallery, for example, has the Queen of Hearts wryly fixed to its reverse.

In the 1520s portrait miniatures began to appear at the French and English courts, often ceremoniously presented by monarchs as tokens of royal favour. In the circle of Elizabeth I in the 1580s, the wealthy wore her portrait as a display of love and allegiance to their queen. When James I took the throne in 1603, the practice continued with artists like Isaac Oliver (*c.*1565-1617) and, most famously, the miniaturist Nicholas Hilliard (*c.*1547-1619), under whom Oliver trained. Together they painted numerous miniatures of the royal family, whose portraits are easier to identify than those shown here. The burning men are the rarest, quietly ablaze in the flames of love for eternity in just a handful of collections around the world.

Mapping the Heart (1654)

Follow the map shown here and embark on a journey through a non-existent country, as the various stages of love are imagined as geography through which one must navigate carefully. The Land of Tenderness is a realm of pleasure and peril in equal measure, warns the French writer Madeleine de Scudéry (1607-1701) in her allegorical design of 1654, the first of its kind, and it's only by following the suggested routes that one can be certain of life's reward.

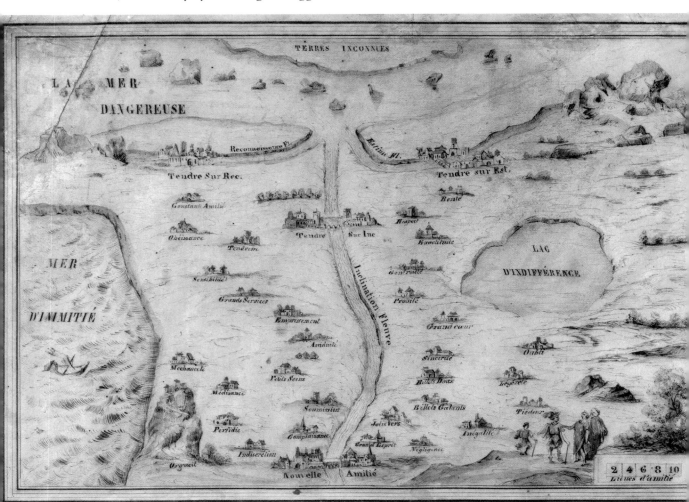

Above: Le Pays de Tendre

Opposite: Map of a Woman's Heart (1840), Joseph Husson.

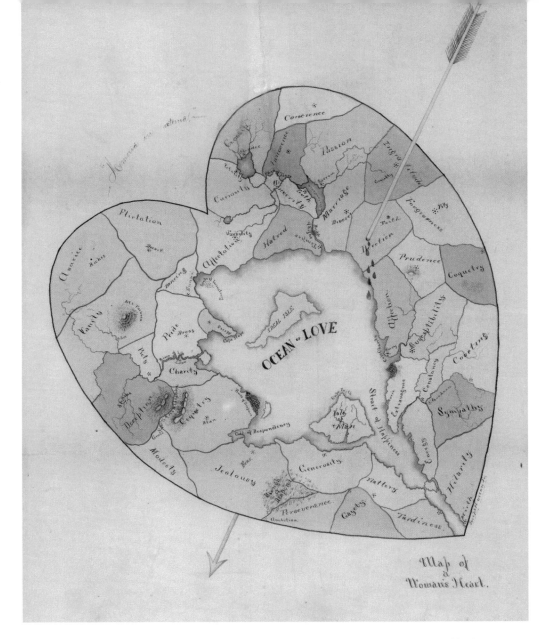

So which path should the amorous take? The setting is framed by three rivers: Recognisance, Esteem and the River of Inclination (each with a town built across it), all of which feed into the Dangerous Sea. The traveller's starting point is at the very south, at New Friendship, where one is faced with a choice of four routes, each passing through a line of settlements. The closer one stays to the central River of Inclination, the more positive the outcome. So, taking the path just to the west of Inclination will take one through Complacency and Small Cares and on to Obedience, Constant Friendship and finally the town of Tender-upon-Recognisance. To the east of Inclination, the young lover will encounter first Great Spirit and Pleasing Verses before passing through Honesty and Respect to reach Tender-upon-Esteem. (One can always switch to the adjacent positive path if so inclined, via the bridge at Tender-upon-Inclination.)

So far, so good – but what awaits those who stray from these noble values? To the far east, Negligence leads to Lukewarmness and ultimately a fall into the Lake of Indifference. Even worse, to the far west we see that Indiscretion leads to Perfidiousness, Mischief and a miserable fate in the Sea of Enmity, joining the vessel sinking beneath its waters.

De Scudéry originally designed the map to accompany her romance novel *Clélie* (1654-61), in which the eponymous heroine is stolen from her lover Aronces by his rival Horatius during an earthquake. But then the map and its courtly concepts became a popular social game, first among the author's genteel literary circle known as 'Les Précieuses', and then with gallant young men who made their own copies on the promise of gaining insight on the woman's perspective into Tenderness. Though 'Les Pécieuses' enjoyed only another five years of popular admiration before Molière's savage comedy of manners *Les Précieuses ridicules* made them the tittering-stock of France, the tradition of allegorically mapping lands of love, marriage, and the terrain of the heart has continued to this day, providing us with some of the most beautiful examples of pictorial cartography ever drawn.

Right: The Sea of Matrimony (1906), *a pocket map for the newlywed to safely sail the route from Honeymoon Island through First Quarrel Reef, past Cape Henpeck, to Little Blessings, Comfort Cove and ultimately Mt. Joy.*

Following Spread: Geographical Guide to a Man's Heart with Obstacles and Entrances Clearly Marked; *and* Geographical Guide to a Woman's Heart Emphasizing Points of Interest to the Romantic Traveler *by Jo Lowry, 1960.*

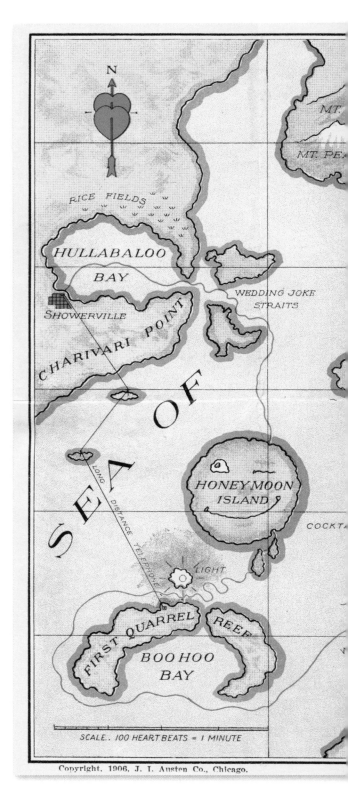

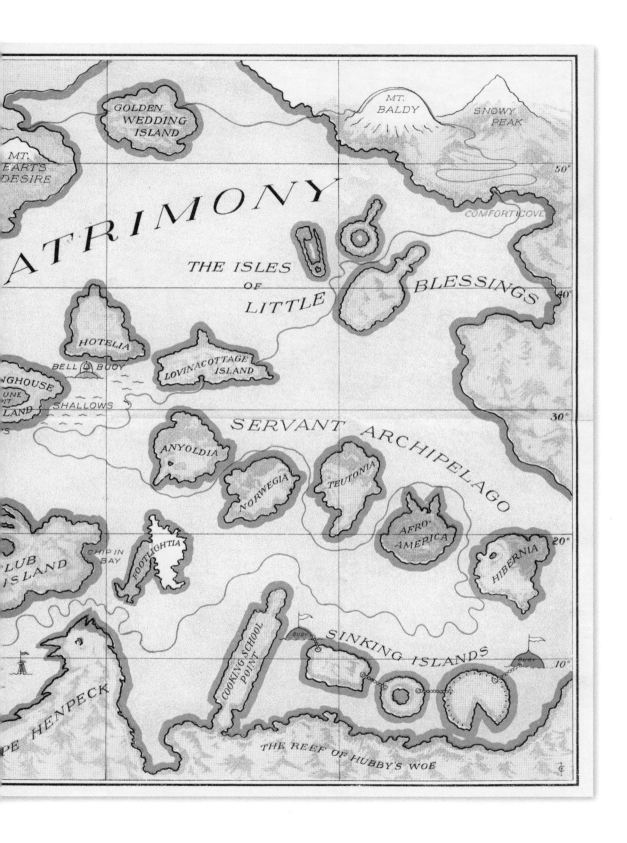

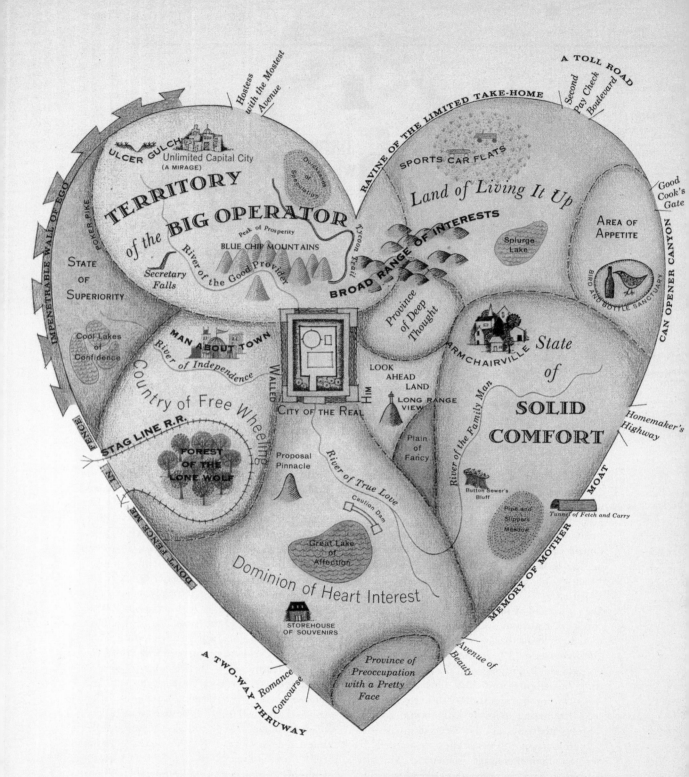

GEOGRAPHICAL GUIDE TO A
MAN'S HEART
with obstacles and entrances clearly marked

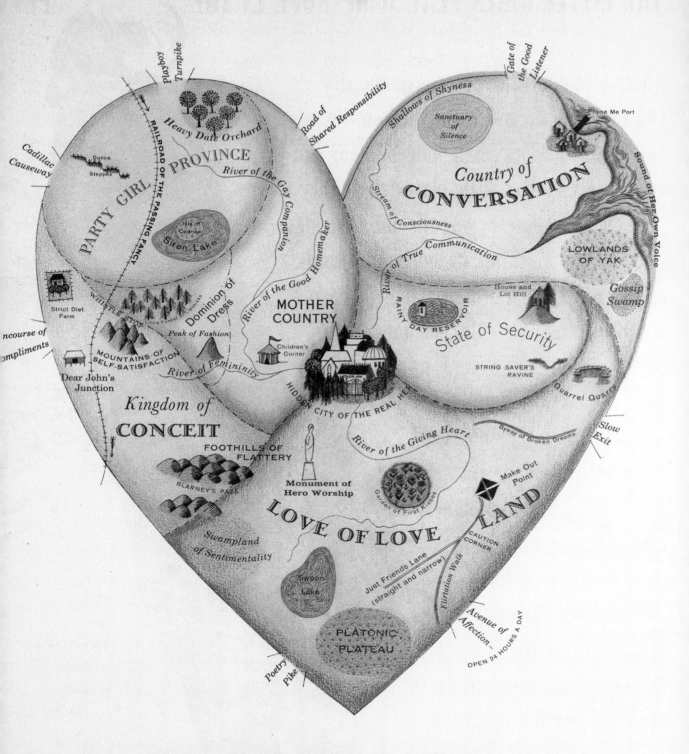

GEOGRAPHICAL GUIDE TO A
WOMAN'S HEART
emphasizing points of interest to the romantic traveler

Lovers' Eyes, and Other Love Tokens

Some of the most powerful objects in museum collections can be the smallest. Objects given as tokens of love, for example, can be the size of a thimble or a penny, yet represent an entire lifetime spent by two people together. Love tokens are not of course a recent invention, nor are they unique to Western tradition. In ancient China, for example, they took the form of hairpins, mirrors and combs, the latter tied to the beautiful Chinese idiom '*Bai tou xie lao*', meaning the happy couple will be together until their hair turns white. Another loving gift was of pepper to be shared by a new couple, the many seeds representing the hope for many children. Rouge boxes were broken in half, with one lover keeping the lid and the other the body. The unintended advantage of this was that, years later, separated families were sometimes identified and reunited through the rejoining of the pieces given by their ancestors.

A Chinese 'love token' jade and gold comb, made and gifted during the Eastern Han dynasty (AD 25-220).

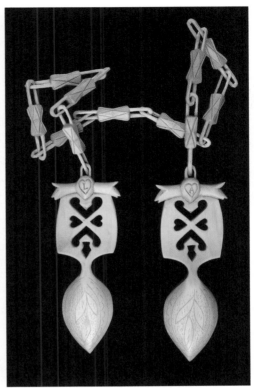

Left: a Welsh lovespoon; Above: a set of carved chained wedding spoons for a pair of newlyweds.

In Wales, the gifting of a carved lovespoon, like that shown above, by a young man attempting to impress a girl with his woodworking skills, is an art of long tradition, with the oldest surviving example dating to 1667. From the early nineteenth century, a similar tradition in sprang up in Norway.

For long-distance couples wishing to hold some personalised, tangible reminder of their bond, love tokens fashioned from everyday coins in circulation offered a cheap and easy memento, that one could keep in the pocket or hold in the palm of the hand. Simply sand off the details from one or both faces (as we have seen done with the convict coins of page 143), and re-engrave with the initials of your loved one, adding extra decorative detail if you possess sufficient skill. This fashion reached its height in the 1800s when sentimentality was at a particular high in England, with Queen Victoria's public mourning for her late husband Albert, but surviving examples date back to at least the 1600s, when folk artists would 'pin-punch' (using a hammer and pin), to make crude engravings on coins. At the same time in France much more artful love tokens were in official use, in the form of treizains, or marriage medals, which were blessed by the priest during the ceremony.

Above: An 1841 thaler of German or Austrian design, re-engraved with the initials of a loved one in the 1880s or 1890s to form a love token.

Above: A love token made from a bun penny (bronze pre-decimal penny (1d) issued by the Royal Mint from 1860 to 1894), beautifully engraved for 'Alice'.

But perhaps the strangest small gifts passed between lovers were the painted 'lovers' eyes' (see pages 158-59) miniatures of the eighteenth and early nineteenth centuries, produced as romantic souvenirs in a time when it was most uncouth to perform any public display of affection. This art of rendering the magical power of a gaze on pieces of ivory and porcelain small enough to be secreted on one's person is said to have begun with the infatuation of the Prince of Wales – later to be King George IV – for the twice-widowed Maria Fitzherbert. Despite the fact that at twenty-seven she was six years older than him, as well as being a Catholic and a commoner, George obsessed over her and threatened suicide if he could not have her. He proposed, and in response Fitzherbert fled the country. She soon received a letter from George, containing a small miniature painting of his right eye, done by

Right: A small ink-and-watercolour love token thought to have been made c.1800 in Harrisburg, Pennsylvania, USA.

his friend the master miniaturist Richard
Cosway. 'If you have not totally forgotten
the whole countenance,' he wrote to
her, 'I think the likeness will strike
you.' Fitzherbert soon returned to
England, secretly married George,
and reciprocated his gift with an
eye miniature of her own. The
story spurred a fashion for eye
miniature gift-giving in English
courting couples, with eyes painted
on brooches and other jewellery, on
toothpick and snuff boxes, usually
also containing locks of hair.

*A Dutch boxwood love
token snuff box, dated
1767, and carved
with the figures of a
lion, a mer-lion and
mer-demon, with a man
and woman embracing
on the cover.*

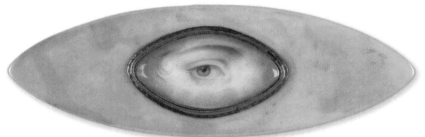

Above: An eye miniature painted onto an elliptical ivory box, c.1800.

Right: A later example of an eye miniature, painted c.1900.

Above: Watercolour on ivory, Eye of 'Maria Miles Heyward', c.1802.

Below: An eye brooch of the early nineteenth century.

Left: Lover's eyes c.1840, with a lock of hair.

Left: A watercolour and gouache eye miniature, inscribed 'Ann Fryer 30th June 1787'.

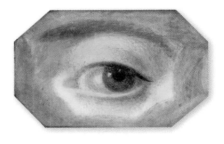

Above: Eye miniature of before 1837.

Left: The eye of Princess Charlotte of Wales, 1796-1817, by the artist Charlotte Jones.

Above: Eye miniature attributed to William Charles Ross (1794-1860).

Above: A portrait of an eye mounted as a ring.

Elizabeth Blackwell's
A Curious Herbal *(1737-9)*

'Behind every great man is a great woman', goes the saying, but of course this is also true of some pretty feckless (or perhaps more kindly, hapless) men too, whose ill fortunes are persistently turned around by a more capable spouse. For the Scottish artist and writer Elizabeth Blackwell (1707-58), the misfortune to whom she was devoted was her cousin Alexander Blackwell (1709-47), whom she had secretly married in Aberdeen while he was studying to be a physician at Marischal College. There was no doubting the quality of education the multilingual Blackwell had received, but it transpired that, having eloped with Elizabeth before completing his studies, his qualifications to practise medicine were questionable. When those questions began to be asked, the Blackwells beat a fast path to London before any charges could be brought.

In London, Alexander tried his hand at printing, working first as a proofreader for William Wilkins, before charging off to start up his own printing company in the Strand despite possessing next-to-no knowledge of the workings of the industry. ('There are few more impressive sights than a Scotsman on the make,' once quipped J. M. Barrie.) This to the contempt of the other local print houses, who found it outrageous Blackwell had performed no apprenticeship nor joined the printers' guild. In breach of strict trade laws, his business tanked, and he was left with overwhelming debts and thrown into debtor's prison.

Elizabeth had watched helplessly as her husband's spending had detonated the family's prospects, and now as he languished behind bars, she was forced to take on the job of earning enough to provide for the family, save their home and buy her husband out of prison … but how? Her ingenuity found the solution in botany. At that time there was an influx of new plant species arriving in London, brought back by explorers of the New World. The samples were cultivated at horticultural institutions

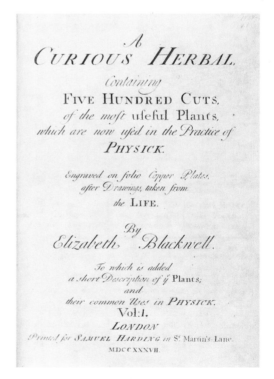

Above: Title page from Elizabeth Blackwell's A Curious Herbal.

Opposite: Plate 269, the Dracontium, from A Curious Herbal.

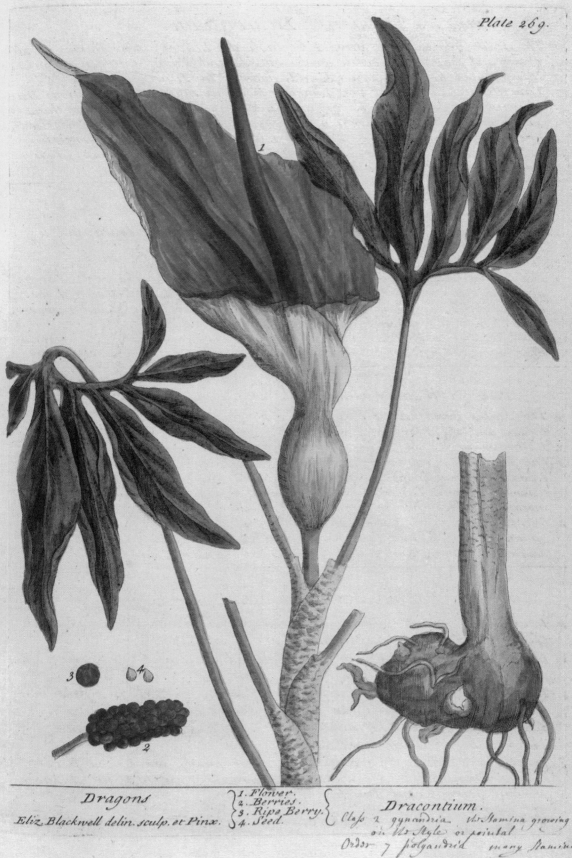

Plate 269.

Dragons

Eliz Blackwell delin. sculp. et Pinx.

1. Flower.
2. Berries.
3. Ripe Berry.
4. Seed.

Dracontium.

Class 2 gynandria the stamina growing
on the Style or pointal
Order 7 polyandria many stamina

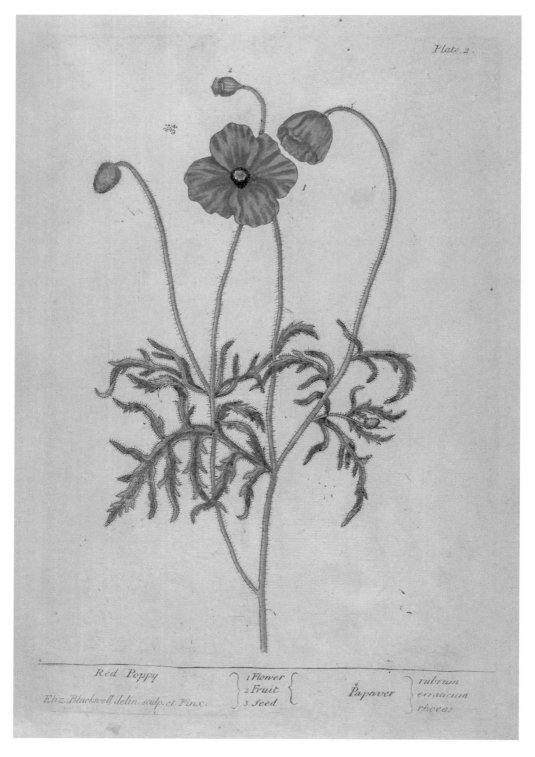

Plate 2, Red Poppy, *from* A Curious Herbal.

Plate 54, Hollyhocks, from A Curious Herbal.

like the Chelsea Physick Garden, and there was a great demand for a herbal (an illustrated scientific compendium) that gathered these natural treasures together for reference.

With the sympathetic co-operation of Isaac Rand, curator of the Chelsea Physick Garden, Elizabeth studied each plant in person to produce five hundred detailed drawings that would form a book titled *A Curious Herbal; containing five Hundred Cuts of the most useful Plants which are now used in the Practice of Physick*. For the titles and annotations she needed the assistance of an expert, and so brought each sketch to her husband in his cell, who would provide the names and translations in Dutch, German, Greek, Italian, Latin and Spanish. Elizabeth then performed the immensely impressive technical feat of engraving each copper printing plate from the five hundred drawings herself. When the first publishing run of the books was completed, she coloured each illustration by hand.

The first *Curious Herbal* was a critical success – the Swedish botanist Carl Linnaeus admiringly nicknamed her 'Botanica Blackwellia' – and the profits were sufficient to pay off Alexander's debts and secure his release. Old habits soon returned, though, and his debts again began to build up. Elizabeth was forced to sell a portion of the publishing rights of the book, and after further business enterprises failed, Alexander left his family for Sweden, where he somehow managed to secure hia appointment as court physician to

King Frederick I. His ambition was once again his downfall, as he took it upon himself to act as British ambassador and sent communiqués to a Danish minister to strengthen diplomatic relations with Sweden. This was seen as conspiracy against Frederick. Alexander was beheaded on 9 August 1747, reportedly after light-heartedly apologising for placing his head on the wrong side of the block, explaining that it was his first beheading.

Ladies of the Night – Harris's List of Covent-Garden Ladies *(1757-95)*

Were you to have taken an ill-advised midnight stroll through the seedier parts of late eighteenth-century London, you might well have encountered the impressively vast figure of Francis Grose (1731-91) compiling his collection of common slang, *A Classical Dictionary of the Vulgar Tongue* (1785). Armed only with a notebook and a nervous assistant, Grose was fearless in his social spelunking of docks, bars and brothels in pursuit of crude and criminal shorthand – the kind of vocabulary omitted from Dr Johnson's dictionary. This turned up terms like 'burning shame, a lighted candle stuck into the private parts of a woman' (to which Grose annotated in his own copy: 'certainly not intended by Nature for a candlestick'); as well as 'fun thruster, a Sodomite', and 'apple dumpling shop, a woman's bosom', among others.[1]

One set of phrases in the *Dictionary of the Vulgar Tongue* concerns a particular area of London: 'COVENT GARDEN AGUE, the venereal disease', wrote Grose, 'COVENT GARDEN ABBESS, a bawd [madam of a brothel]'; COVENT GARDEN NUN, a prostitute'. Covent Garden was a notorious hub of prostitution in the eighteenth century, and its nightly male wanderers, possessed of less academic interests than Grose, were assisted by a guide of their own. *Harris's List of Covent-Garden Ladies* was a pocketbook of around 150 pages printed annually between 1757 and 1795, cataloguing the 120 to 190 prostitutes working in the Covent Garden and West End areas of the city. Around 8,000 copies were sold annually for two shillings and sixpence each, but its author was never discovered (although Samuel Derrick, a Grub

Street hack, and a Covent Garden pimp named Jack Harris, are commonly identified as likely culprits).

The frontispiece illustration from the 1793 edition.

---

1 Some more of those others include:
beard splitter, a man much given to wenching.
blowsabella, a woman whose hair is dishevelled and hanging about her face.
casting up one's accounts, vomiting.
cup of the creature, a cup of good liquor.
duke of limbs, a tall, awkward, ill-made fellow.
frenchified, infected with venereal disease.
puff guts, a fat man.
slubber de gullion, a dirty nasty fellow.

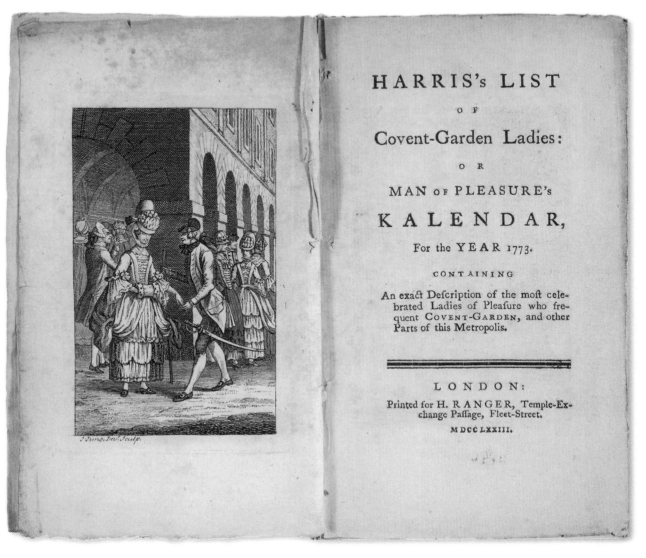

HARRIS's LIST

OF

Covent-Garden Ladies:

OR

MAN OF PLEASURE's

KALENDAR,

For the YEAR 1773.

CONTAINING

An exact Defcription of the moſt celebrated Ladies of Pleaſure who frequent COVENT-GARDEN, and other
Parts of this Metropolis.

LONDON:

Printed for H. RANGER, Temple-Ex-
change Paſſage, Fleet-Street.

MDCCLXXIII.

Title page of the 1773 edition.

What makes the lurid *List* so interesting to browse is the information we learn of these ladies of the second half of the eighteenth century – not just their names, ages and physical attributes, but their specialities and talents both in and out of the bedroom (including their singing and dancing skills), their quirks of personality and snatches of personal background. The 'genteel agreeable' Miss B—nd of No. 28 Frith Street listed in the 1788 edition, for example, is 'distinguished more by the elegancy of her dress, than the beauty of her person, which might perhaps have been ranked in the list of tolerable's, had not the small-pox been quite so unkind; she is, nevertheless, a desirable well tempered piece'.

Miss Davenport's entry concludes: 'Her teeth are remarkably fine; she is tall, and so well proportioned (when you examine her whole naked figure, which she will permit you to do, if you perform the Cytherean Rites like an able priest) that she might be taken for a fourth Grace, or a breathing animated Venus de Medicis'. Miss Clicamp, of No. 2 York Street

The Cov.t Garden Morning Frolick

Invented & Engrav'd by L. P. Boitard. Publish'd According to Act of Parliam.t Oct.r 9. 1747. Price one Shilling.

near Middlesex Hospital, is noted as 'one of the finest, fattest figures as fully finished for fun and frolick as fertile fancy ever formed … fortunate for the true lovers of fat, should fate throw them into the possession of such full grown beauties.'

Eventually, however, the same shift in public attitudes to indecency that saw Grose expurgate his *Vulgar Tongue* also led to a more robust intolerance of the sex trade and calls for reform, and the 1795 edition of *Harris's List*, the crudest of all, was the last to be put out, as those responsible for its printing were fined and imprisoned.

Above: The Covt: Garden Morning Frolick *(1747) by Louis Philippe Boitard, a satire on the drunken chaos of the brothel-filled Covent Garden Piazza, with the notorious courtesan Bet Careless shown asleep in the sedan chair.*

Opposite and *Following Pages:* The Bed *(1893) and* In Bed, the Kiss *(1892), two intimate studies of female prostitutes by Henri de Toulouse-Lautrec. Lautrec was commissioned by a Paris brothel on the rue d'Ambroise Part to decorate its walls with painted panels, and between 1892 and 1895 produced hundreds of artworks of the women's lives.*

Baretia Bonafidia – *the Extraordinary Love Story of Jeanne Baret* (1766)

The desiccated plant specimen shown here is *Turraea Rutilans*, of the Turraea genus of plants native throughout the Old World Tropics, including Madagascar and Mauritius. Botanically speaking the small green shrub isn't particularly special, but its original name of *Baretia Bonafidia*, given by the French naturalist Philibert Commerson (1727-73), leads us down a rabbit hole of history starring an exceptional woman all but forgotten.

In 1766 it had been three years since the kingdoms of Great Britain, France and Spain, with Portugal in agreement, came together to sign the Treaty of Paris, thereby formally ending the Seven Years' War. French pride remained bruised and national funds were still recovering, when Louis-Antoine de Bougainville (1729-1811) proposed leading the first French circumnavigation of the world. Bougainville left Nantes on 15 November 1766 with an expedition of two vessels, the *Boudeuse* and the *Étoile* (commanded by François Chenard de la Giraudais). This was a large expedition, with crews of 214 and 116 respectively, and notable for the unprecedented emphasis on its scientific nature, with an astronomer, an engineer and Commerson on board, who with his personal valet and mountains of equipment was given the captain's cabin on the *Étoile*.

What none of the crew knew was that the young man accompanying the botanist was actually a woman named Jeanne Baret. She had first entered Commerson's household as a housekeeper, but after the death of his wife their relationship became more intimate, and according to a 'certificate of pregnancy' dated 1764, Baret fell pregnant.

When Commerson was invited to join the expedition in 1765 on the recommendation of the Paris Academy of Sciences, he hesitated

to accept the prestigious position; he was in poor health, and Baret was both managing his household and acting as his full-time nurse. At some point, though, the couple dreamt up the scheme to disguise Baret as a young man, so that she could join the expedition and tend to him during the journey. This was an immensely dangerous plan. The hazards of oceanic navigation were the least of their concerns – regulations forbade any woman to step aboard ship, and there was immense superstition among European sailors that women brought bad luck at sea. The biggest concern, of course, was that she would be the only woman in an all-male crew of hundreds, and if she were discovered there was no telling what would happen. Baret knew her discovery would be catastrophic but proceeded regardless in order to take care of Commerson.

During the journey Commerson was struck with terrible seasickness, as well as an ulcer on his leg, and Baret spent most of her time caring for him in their private quarters, which included a latrine for their private use. Only after landing at Montevideo did their official duties began, but with Commerson crippled by his injury it was Baret who performed the arduous tasks, carrying the equipment, collecting samples and performing surveys. At Rio de Janeiro, Commerson was in such pain that he was confined to quarters, so Baret joined the landing party. Despite the fact that the expedition's chaplain was murdered by locals soon after coming ashore, Baret pushed on to collect samples, including that of a beautiful flowering vine that would be named Bougainvillea in honour of the mission's leader.

According to Bougainville it was only on their arrival at Tahiti in April 1768 that Baret's true sex was discovered, when a crowd of Tahitians surrounded her, immediately identifying her as a woman, forcing her to return to the ship and the consternation of the

An imagined portrait of Jeanne Baret (1816).

crew. Accounts differ as to what happened next – Bougainville mentions no serious consequences, but another first-hand account reports that Baret was violently assaulted by the men. The couple continued on the voyage across the Pacific, but on arrival at Mauritius (then known as Isle de France), Commerson was excited to discover that the governor of the island was a friend and colleague, Pierre Poivre (1719-86). When Bougainville's expedition headed off, Commerson and Baret remained behind.

From 1770 the couple lived happily on Mauritius for three years, collecting and studying local flora, until Commerson died from his poor health in 1773. Records show that by 1776 Baret had finally made it back to France, completing the journey that established her as the first woman to perform a circumnavigation of the globe. Of the thousands of plant specimens and new discoveries Commerson and Baret recorded together, over seventy are named in Commerson's honour, but none carry Baret's name. The plant shown at the beginning of this chapter was named *Baretia Bonafidia* by Commerson in tribute to his lover, but unfortunately by the time the records of his findings made it back to France, the plant had already been named *Turraea Rutilans* by a colleague. Only in 2012 was her name given to a plant, *Solanum baretiae*, named in her honour by the biologist Eric Tepe of the University of Utah and the University of Cincinnati, upon learning of her airbrushing from history.

Carte Generale de la Terre ou Mappe Monde (1785), one of the most decorative maps of the eighteenth century, by Jean Baptiste Louis Clouet. The routes of Bougainville, as well as those of Magellan, Tasman, Edmond Halley and Captain James Cook, are marked in red.

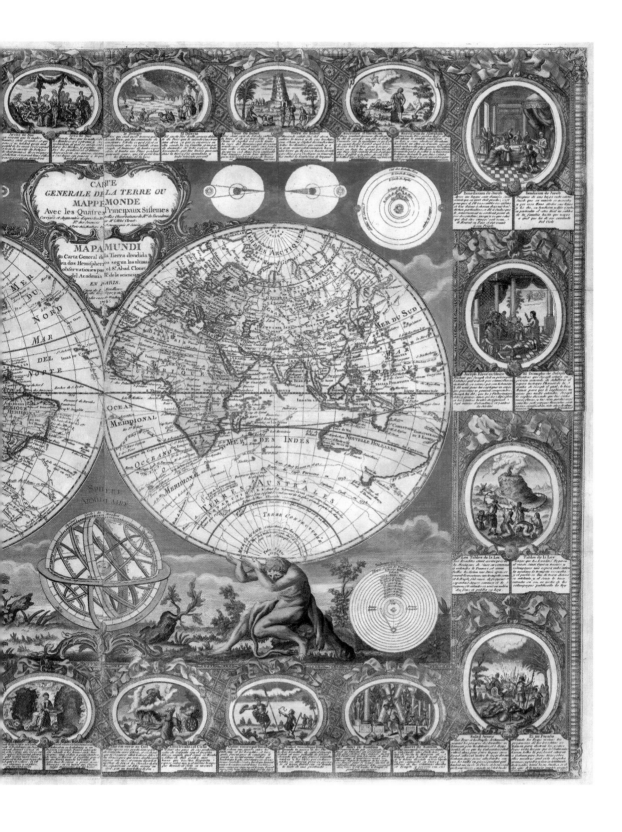

Yoruba Carved Wedding Chain

'Tying the knot', 'getting hitched', 'the old ball and chain' – many cultures around the globe have the idea of marriage as an attachment. In some African cultures long grasses are braided to bind a bride and groom, but in art it's the Yoruba people of West Africa who perhaps illustrate it most strikingly with these carved wedding chains, which are common gifts to newlyweds. The Yoruba, who historically have inhabited large parts of Nigeria, Benin and Togo in a collective region known as Yorubaland, have always been known for their artistic skill with sculpture and carving. This talent is flexed most powerfully in celebration of significant social events, particularly marriage.

In contrast to more sober ceremonial traditions of other cultures, Yoruba weddings remain especially joyous and colourful affairs. Take the 'Je ki'n r'ile oko gbe' prayer for example, which represents the Yoruba belief in blessing a wife's buttocks, that they may sit in the home they share with their spouse for a long time (i.e., not having to live with parents, or move on to a second marriage). In order to effect this blessing in ceremonies, the masters of the ceremony, the Alaga Iduro and Alaga Ijokoo, add to the fun of the service by asking the brides to grab their own buttocks while chanting what is informally known as the 'my bumbum' prayer, in a call-and-response fashion. (Hard to imagine this taking off in the Catholic Church.) There is also what's known as the 'my back, my back' chant, which is a prayer for the bride's ability to have children, which she will eventually carry by strapping them to her back.

The chains shown here feature the figures of a man and woman joined with an 'unending'

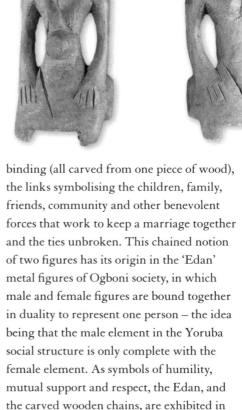

binding (all carved from one piece of wood), the links symbolising the children, family, friends, community and other benevolent forces that work to keep a marriage together and the ties unbroken. This chained notion of two figures has its origin in the 'Edan' metal figures of Ogboni society, in which male and female figures are bound together in duality to represent one person – the idea being that the male element in the Yoruba social structure is only complete with the female element. As symbols of humility, mutual support and respect, the Edan, and the carved wooden chains, are exhibited in museums around the world.

Above: Ogboni Edan staffs, showing a chained male and female figure representing a single person.

Right: A carved Yoruba panel that serves as a summary of family life. In the centre is a copulating couple, representing marriage as necessary to maintain the community. The man is a hunter, judging by his cartridge belt. The tortoise represents the Ifa priest, as he carries an Ifa oracle board on his back.

A carved Yoruba mirror frame, a prestige object popular as a wedding gift. The mating scene at the top is a reminder of the perks of marriage, and the ashe (life force) that strengthens with children.

A wooden belly mask in the shape of a pregnant woman's torso, with the abdomen engraved with geometric scar patterns. The Yoruba consider women to be the stronger sex, but Yoruba mask dancers are always men, even if portraying women, in which chase they widen their hips with sticks and rags, or in this case, with the use of a belly mask.

James Graham and the Celestial Bed (1780), *with Other Love Quacks*

As the instigator of irrational behaviour and inflictor of heartbreak, love was long diagnosed as a physical malady throughout the history of medicine. The eleventh-century physician and monk, Constantine the African, blamed it for the build-up of excess 'black bile' that was believed in medieval Europe to cause melancholia: 'The love that is also called "eros" is a disease touching the brain … Sometimes the cause of this love is an intense natural need to expel a great excess of humours … this illness causes thoughts and worries as the afflicted person seeks to find and possess what they desire.' Near the end of the twelfth century, the physician Gerard of Berry added that lovesickness caused imbalanced constitutions in its victims, who as a result would become obsessed with objects of beauty and desire, and ultimately develop melancholia. Cures prescribed included daylight and garden walks, warm baths with water lilies and violets, a diet of lamb, lettuce and the (poisonous) root of hellebore, the latter a treatment recommended since the days of Hippocrates. To reset the 'black bile', purgatives, laxatives, and bloodletting were also all considered solutions.[1]

---

1 In modern medicine, there is a condition known as 'broken heart syndrome', or more technically 'stress cardiomyopathy', in which there is a sudden temporary weakening of the muscular portion of the heart brought on by an emotional or physical stressor. In Japan the condition is known as 'takotsubo' cardiomyopathy, which comes from the Japanese word *takotsubo* meaning 'octopus trap', as this is the shape the left ventricle of the heart was seen to take on when affected.

The Celestial Bed
with the Rosy Goddess of Health reposing thereon

The grand 'Celestial Bed' of quack James Graham, c.1782.

Sex quacks have offered wilder treatments for men desperate to recapture lost vigour. In early twentieth-century America the scam artist John Romulus Brinkley (1885-1942) amassed millions of dollars from his patented panacea for male ailments, which he performed surgically despite possessing zero medical qualifications. This widely touted, and scarcely believable, treatment consisted of transplanting goat testicles into the human patient's testicular sac, where the foreign gland would usually just be absorbed by the body. The 'goat-gland doctor' found international fame and great wealth, until word spread that patients were dying from infections and he was finally banned from practising medicine. He died penniless, after lawsuits had stripped him of every ill-gotten dollar.[2, 3]

James Graham (1745-94), the notorious love quack of eighteenth-century London, concocted a less invasive but equally fantastical approach to the treatment of love and sexual relationship issues. The catalyst for Graham's spectacular brand of pseudoscience was the electrical experimentation of Benjamin Franklin that he had witnessed while in America. Franklin would broadcast the power of 'the youngest daughter of the sciences', as the English chemist Joseph Priestley (1733-1804) termed electricity, with public demonstrations that became the entertainment of salons everywhere. This included 'electricity parties', one of which Franklin advertised with: 'A turkey is to be killed for dinner by the electric shock, and roasted by the electric jack, before a fire kindled by the electrified

Bloodletting could relieve the humoral imbalance of the lovesick individual – from Aldobrandino of Siena's Le Régime du corps, 1265.

'Dr' John R. Brinkley, an American quack of the early twentieth century who made millions by transplanting goat testicles into desperate impotent men.

2 Brinkley's testicular treatment has a precursor in the work of the Mauritian physiologist Charles-Édouard Brown-Séquard (1817-94), who at the age of seventy-two reported 'rejuvenated sexual prowess' after performing 'subcutaneous injection of extracts of monkey testis' on himself. (He had the reputation of an eccentric ever since he swallowed the vomit of a Cholera patient during an outbreak in 1853 in order to contract the disease himself and find a cure.) He further claimed, at a meeting of the Société de biologie in Paris, that a hypodermic injection of a fluid sourced from guinea pig testicles resulted in rejuvenation and could prolong human life. 'The lecture must be seen as further proof of the necessity of retiring professors who have attained their threescore and ten years,' wrote a journalist for one Vienna medical publication.

3 And if only to complete a pair of testicular footnotes to dangle at the bottom of this page, it should be noted that the potency of testicles has been respected since antiquity. Pliny recommends athletes chew lamb testicles before a race for a boost, while the ancient Assyrians enshrined men's testicular protection from women into law. From the Code of the Assyrians: 'If a woman in a quarrel injure the testicle of a man, one of her fingers they shall cut off. And if a physician bind it up and the other testicle which is beside it be infected thereby, or take harm; or in a quarrel she injure the other testicle, they shall destroy both of her eyes.'

bottle.' European viewers were also in awe of these attractions of electrical phenomena. Aristocrats threw their own electrical soirées in which they zapped each other with electrified kisses. In France, King Louis XV appointed a court electrician, Jean Abbe Nollet, to invent electrical displays, one of which involved electrocuting a row of several hundred monks, causing them to simultaneously leap into the air.

Graham saw all of this and realised there was money to be made out of the desperate wealthy. Though he'd studied medicine at Edinburgh University he'd left without a degree, and after setting up practices first in Pontefract, Yorkshire, then Bristol and Bath, he came to London and in 1780 opened his Temple of Health in Pall Mall. There he boasted of his 'medico-electrical apparatus', which he advertised as the 'largest, most stupendous, most useful, and most magnificent, that now is, or ever was, in the World'. On stepping into the entrance hall of the Temple, visitors passed piles of walking sticks, crutches, eyeglasses and ear trumpets that they were told had been discarded by previous customers cured by Graham's treatments. Some visited to be cured, others came just to marvel at the electrical machines and conductors, the electrical throne on glass pillars, the statues, paintings, stained glass windows, music, perfumes and the two gigantic 'footmen' called Gog and Magog. Graham gave lectures on the secrets to a happy sex life, livening his performances with a backdrop of barely clothed young models in classical poses as goddesses of health – including, according to legend, a young Emma Lyon, later to become Lady Hamilton. Each lecture was ended by giving the audience an electrical shock via their seats, and then a 'spirit' would burst from a hidden trapdoor, wielding a bottle of patented 'aetherial balsam' to be distributed to the guests.

Dr James Graham Going Along the North Bridge in a High Wind, *a caricature portrait of James Graham by John Kay (1742-1826).*

The grand feature of the Temple, though, was Graham's magnificent mechanical 'celestial bed' (illustrated on page 178). Standing on forty pillars of coloured glass 'of the most exquisite workmanship', the bed had mechanisms that routinely sprayed perfumes of flowers and spices, and various magnets and electrical machines that caused it to hum, electrified with a restorative charge. With its adjustable frame, the bed could be set at various angles, and automata moved about it as music played, reportedly matching the tempo to the exercise of those between its sheets. Conception was guaranteed: 'Any gentleman and his lady desirous of progeny, and wishing to spend an evening in this Celestial apartment … may, by a compliment of a fifty pound bank note be permitted to partake of the heavenly joys it affords,' Graham wrote. 'The barren

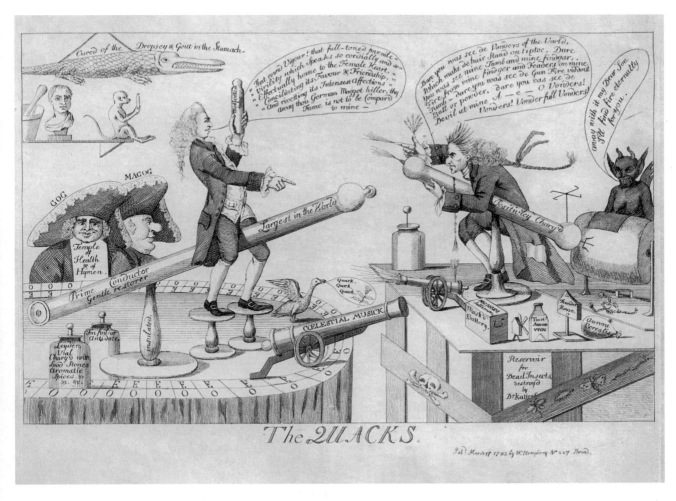

The Quacks. London: W. Humphrey, 17 March 1783. James Graham and Gustavus Katerfelto.

certainly must become fruitful when they are powerfully agitated in the delight.'

The temple attracted large crowds, with the diarist Henry Angelo (1756-1835) visiting incognito. Horace Walpole also paid a visit on 23 August 1780 and described Graham's spectacle as 'the most impudent puppet-show of imposition I ever saw, and the mountebank himself the dullest of his profession, except that he makes the spectators pay a crown apiece'. Every novelty loses its lustre, however. Graham began to run up debts; in 1782 his property was seized and he spent his last years as a travelling lecturer, giving up medical electricity for natural cures (which were no doubt easier to sell). The man labelled by the

The Quacks. London: W. Humphrey, 17 March 1783. James Graham and Gustavus Katerfelto. A caricature of the two most infamous quacks of the day facing off – on the left, James Graham, standing on the glass pillars used in his experiments with electricity; while on the right crouches the Prussian quack and conjurer Gustavus Katterfelto (1743-99), shooting sparks from his fingers conducted from the grindstone being worked by the Devil.

British Medical Journal as 'one of the vilest impostors in the history of quackery', who boasted of possessing the secret of living to the age of 150, died suddenly on his forty-ninth birthday on 23 June 1794, and was buried in Greyfriars churchyard, Edinburgh.

Giacomo Casanova's
History of My Life *(1794)*

'Ultimate sleazeball or tortured romantic?' mused a *Guardian* article in April 2022 of Giacomo Girolamo Casanova, neatly summarising just two of the complicated contradictions of character one finds in the biography of the world's most renowned lothario, who claimed to have seduced 132 women in his lifetime. Whatever your impressions of Casanova, there is a lot more to the man and his story than his modern reputation allows.

Born in Venice to two Venetian actors, Casanova grew up in a city of pleasure, amid its gambling houses, brothels and famed annual Carnival. Effectively abandoned as a young child with his mother away on tour and his father dying when he was eight years old, he was taken into the care of his primary instructor Abbé Gozzi and entered the University of Padua with a keen intellect that soaked up everything from moral philosophy and mathematics to medicine. Gambling debts forced him to leave, however, and he took up a post with the first of many patrons, a seventy-six-year-old Venetian senator who promptly turfed a young Casanova out of his house when he caught him in a dalliance with a young actress that the senator himself fancied. We next find Casanova working as a scribe for Cardinal Acquaviva in Rome, writing love letters for other cardinals, until he was ejected from that too and decided to buy for himself a military commission. He joined a Venetian regiment in Corfu but found the pace of military life too slow and dull and spent his time gambling away his pay. All this, before the age of twenty-one.

Good fortune came in the form of the powerful Bragadin family, who took him in for the next few years after he saved one of their elderly members by countering the family doctor and ordering the removal of

Above: Medallion portrait of Casanova, drawn live in March 1788 by Johann Berka.

Opposite: The first page of Giacomo Casanova's manuscript memoir.

Histoire de ma vie
jusqu'à l'an 1797

Nequicquam sapit qui sibi non sapit
Cic: ad Treb:

Préface

Je commence par déclarer à mon lecteur que dans tout ce que j'ai fait de bon ou de mauvais dans toute ma vie, je suis sûr d'avoir mérité ou démérite, et que par conséquent je dois me croire libre. La doctrine des Stoïciens, et de toute autre secte sur la force du Destin est une chimere de l'imagination qui tient à l'athéisme. Je suis non seulement monothéiste, mais chrétien fortifié par la philosophie, qui n'a jamais rien gâté.

Je crois à l'existence d'un Dieu immatériel auteur..., et maître de toutes les formes; et ce qui me prouve que je n'en ai jamais douté, c'est que j'ai toujours compté sur sa providence, recourant à lui par le moyen de la prière dans toutes mes détresses; et me trouvant toujours exaucé. Le désespoir tue; la prière le fait disparoître; et après elle l'homme confie, et agit. Quels soyent les moyens, dont l'Être des êtres se sert pour détourner les malheurs imminens sur ceux qui implorent son secours, c'est une recherche au dessus du pouvoir de l'entendement de l'homme, qui dans le même instant qu'il contemple l'incomprehensibilité de la providence divine, se voit réduit à l'adorer. Notre ignorance devient notre seule ressource; et les vrais heureux sont ceux qui la chérissent. Il faut donc prier Dieu, et croire d'avoir obtenu la grace, même quand l'apparence nous dit que nous ne l'avons pas obtenu. Pour ce qui regarde la posture du corps dans la quelle il faut être quand on adresse des vœux au créateur, un vers du

A print from 1872 of Casanova demonstrating a French condom to a group of ladies, who laugh at the inflated shape.

a mercury ointment, which he knew to be toxic, from the man's chest. Casanova worked as the nobleman's assistant, dressing magnificently and tumbling further into his by now well-established vices of gambling and philandering. Then two simultaneous scandals erupted: a young girl accused him of rape; and a bizarre prank in which he dug up a recently buried corpse to scare a friend backfired, when the target of the joke went into nervous shock and remained paralysed.

Casanova fled Venice for Parma, where he fell deeply in love with a Frenchwoman he calls 'Henriette' in his autobiography *Histoire de ma vie* (The Story of My Life). 'They who believe that a woman is incapable of making a man equally happy all the twenty-four hours of the day have never known an Henriette,' he wrote. 'The joy which flooded my soul was far greater when I conversed with her during the day than when I held her in my arms at night. Having read a great deal and having natural taste, Henriette judged rightly of everything.' Her sensible judgement extended also to Casanova – Henriette abandoned him, breaking his heart, although kindly leaving him a token sum to help with his finances.

From here, in about 1750, his lascivious reputation is built as he heads off on a grand tour, to Lyon and Paris, Prague and Vienna, attempting to mend a broken heart by seducing every woman in sight, to the point where police forces of each city would make note of his prolific amorous affairs and the scandals that ensued. When he finally returned to Venice, it wasn't long before he found himself arrested for affront to religion and common decency and was thrown into 'The Leads', a seven-celled prison in the Doge's palace reserved for high-status prisoners.

Following these formative episodes, his *Histoire de ma vie* continues for hundreds more pages of Netflixian drama at breakneck pace: a prison break involving a secret tunnel, a renegade priest and a bedsheet rope; a return to Paris and a renewed, rampant schedule of seductions; his role as a trustee in the first state lottery, earning him a fortune; his duping of French high society with his extensive knowledge of the occult; more debts; espionage missions; more prison arrests; repeated and crippling bouts of venereal disease that must have surprised absolutely no one; expulsion from Warsaw after a mutually destructive pistol duel with a Polish colonel over the affections of an Italian actress; and dodging assassination in Barcelona. Finally, in 1785, Casanova took up a position as librarian to Count Joseph Karl von Waldstein, a chamberlain of the emperor, in the Castle of Dux, Bohemia (now the Czech Republic). Hated by the other castle inhabitants, he led a rather lonely existence with only fox terriers for company, focusing entirely on completing his memoirs which he achieved before his death in 1798.

Casanova writes of his ideal liaison involving much more than just sex; there had to be a plot. He developed a seductive formula. Act I: find an attractive woman with a brutish or jealous partner. Act II: improve her situation. Act III: in her gratitude she would be seduced and a thrilling affair would begin. Act IV: he loses interest, declares his unworthiness and arranges for her a worthy replacement, and exit. 'There is no honest woman with an uncorrupted heart whom a man is not sure of conquering by dint of gratitude,' he wrote. 'It is one of the surest and shortest means.' Neither alcohol nor violence were to be used; words were all that were needed. 'Without speech, the pleasure of love is diminished by at least two-thirds.' These should be subtle words, however, for 'a man who makes known his love by words is a fool'.

Dream of the Fisherman's Wife *(1814) and the Erotic Art of Japanese* shunga

Enough to at least give one pause when next presented with a sushi dish, this is *Dream of the Fisherman's Wife* in all its aqua-erotic glory. Also referred to as *Girl Diver and Octopi*, the woodblock print was designed by the famous Japanese artist Hokusai (1760-1849) for his three-volume work *Kinoe no Komatsu* ('Pining for Love'). This title is perhaps the most notorious work of *shunga*, a sexually explicit art style influenced in part by Chinese medical manuals from the Muromachi era (1336 to 1573), and Tang Dynasty artists like Zhou Fang who tended to exaggerate the size of genitals in their illustrations. Literally, *shunga* translates as 'spring' (a euphemism for sex), but also serves as a contraction of *shunkyū̄-higi-ga*, the Japanese pronunciation of a Chinese set of twelve scrolls depicting the twelve sexual acts that the crown prince would perform. In its early days, *shunga* artists drew on stories of scandals that emerged from the Imperial court and monasteries for their material.

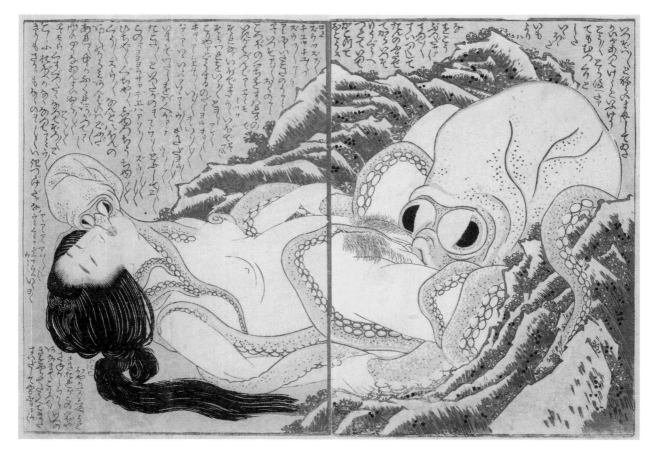

Another example of shunga *by Hokusai, this being* Woman and Young Man Biting Towel, *c.1817.*

Most artists of *ukiyo-e*, the Japanese art style that flourished between the seventeenth and nineteenth centuries, dabbled in *shunga* at some point, but it is Hokusai's *Dream of the Fisherman's Wife* that is probably the most famous example. You might well wonder what it is we're seeing. A young *ama* diver is entwined sexually with a pair of octopuses, which would have reminded contemporary viewers of the popular story of Princess Tamatori, a shell diver who searched for a pearl stolen from her husband's family by Ryūjin, the dragon god of the sea. Tamatori dives down to Ryūjin's subaquatic palace, cuts open her own breast and hides the jewel inside. This gives her the power to swim faster and escape, but after reaching the surface she dies from her wound.

In Hokusai's image, the accompanying text sheds light on his scene, with what, I hope, will be the strangest transcript you'll read this week:

LARGE OCTOPUS: *'My wish comes true at last, this day of days; finally I have you in my grasp! Your 'bobo' is ripe and full, how wonderful! Superior to all others! To suck and suck and suck some more. After we do it masterfully, I'll guide you to the Dragon Palace of the Sea God and envelop you …'*

MAIDEN: *'You hateful octopus! Your sucking at the mouth of my womb makes me gasp for breath! Aah! Yes … it's … there!!! With the sucker, the sucker!! Inside, squiggle, squiggle, oooh! Oooh,*
good, oooh good! There, there! Theeeeere! Goood! Whew! Aah! Good, good, aaaaaaaaaah! Not yet! Until now it was I that men called an octopus! An octopus! Ooh! Whew! How are you able…!? Ooh!'

LARGE OCTOPUS: *'All eight limbs to entwine with!! How do you like it this way? Ah, look! The inside has swollen, moistened by the warm waters of lust …'*

MAIDEN: *'Yes, it tingles now; soon there will be no sensation at all left in my hips. Ooooooh! Boundaries and borders gone! I've vanished …'*

SMALL OCTOPUS: *'After daddy finishes, I too want to rub and rub my suckers at the ridge of your furry place until you disappear and then I'll suck some more …'*

The *shunga* style peaked in popularity in the Edo period (1603 to 1867), and with improvements in woodblock printing techniques, was produced in dramatically greater quantity and quality. The Japanese government repeatedly attempted to ban *shunga* throughout its history, though as it turned out it wasn't censorship but the rise of erotic photography that would all but put an end to the art.

The Erotic Picture Book of Snow on Fuji (1824) starts innocently enough with an eponymously snowy scene, but things soon take a passionate turn for the heroine. By the Japanese ukiyo-e artist Keisai Eisen, whose ōkubi-e ('large head pictures'), are considered to be masterpieces of the Bunsei Era (1818-30).

Percy Shelley's Wandering Heart, and Other Post-Mortem Keepsakes

Here's a quiz question to raise at the next lull in conversation at a family meal: what common feature links the rotten, putrefied corpses of Henry I, Eleanor of Castile, Frédéric Chopin, and Thomas Hardy? The answer is that each is missing its heart, removed post-mortem so that it could be buried in a separate place to the body.

Historically the practice of 'heart burial' (and the related fashion of separately interring the entrails and viscera) was most popular in medieval Europe, in tandem with the rise in popularity of courtly love and the belief that the essence of a person resided in the heart. For royalty, divided burial locations were either purely political or often a balance between obligations of duty and a personal love for a homeland or favoured escape. The body of Henry I (c.1068-1135) was interred at Reading Abbey, England, while his heart, bowels, brains, eyes and tongue were interred at Rouen Cathedral, France. The body of Eleanor of Castile (1241-90), first wife of Edward I, was granted a triple burial: her viscera were buried in Lincoln Cathedral, her body at Westminster Abbey, and her heart at the Dominican priory at Blackfriars (together with that of her son Alphonso), in an elaborate monument that featured wall paintings and statues.

Through the centuries the practice became rarer, but still occurred. Napoleon ordered that on his death his heart be sent to his wife Marie Louise (while his penis was, according

When the lead coffin of the seventeenth-century French noblewoman Louise de Quengo, Lady of Brefeillac, was excavated in 2013, she was found to have been buried with the embalmed heart of her husband, the knight Toussaint de Perrien. Louise's own heart is missing and has not been found, although it is thought to have been removed and placed in her husband's grave. The inscription on the lead cardiotaph, or heart urn, reads: 'Here lies the heart of Toussaint de Perrien, Knight of Brefeillac, whose body lies near Carhaix in the Discalced Carmelite Convent, which he founded, and who died in Rennes on August 30, 1649.'

A lock of hair of Percy Bysshe Shelley, and another of Mary Shelley, held within the front doublure, or decorative book lining, of this c.1822 volume of manuscript letters. The rear doublure (shown below) contains what are supposedly some of Percy Bysshe Shelley's ashes, collected by Edward Trelawny from the beach near Viareggio.

to legend, removed by his priest as a keepsake).[1] In accordance with his dying wish, the heart of Chopin (1810-49) was removed and preserved in a jar of brandy. His sister smuggled the pickled heart back to his Polish homeland, where it was sealed within a pillar of Warsaw's Holy Cross Church beneath an inscription from Matthew 6:21: 'For where your treasure is, there will your heart be also.'

The fate of the heart of Thomas Hardy (1840-1928) is slightly stranger. The writer had wished for his body to be buried at Stinsford in the same grave as his first wife, Emma, but it was decided that he should instead be interred in Westminster Abbey's Poets' Corner. As a compromise his heart was buried with Emma at Stinsford, but according to rumour a cat got at it the night before the burial and chewed it to pieces. The story goes that the cat was grabbed and thrown in the grave along with the remaining fragments.

Sometimes a lover's heart wasn't buried but kept as a memento. These kinds of physical reminders weren't so unusual, especially in the Victorian era. Teeth and locks of hair were

---

1 Napoleon's penis, which enjoys its own Wikipedia page, has a wild ride of a provenance trail. Previous owners include the legendary bookdealer A. S. W. Rosenbach (1876-1952) who bought the 'mummified tendon taken from Napoleon's body during the post-mortem' from Maggs Bros, London, in 1924. In 1927 it was exhibited at New York City's Museum of French Art, where a *Time* journalist compared it to a 'maltreated strip of buckskin shoelace', and another visitor thought it more like a 'shriveled eel'. The humiliation continued with the *New York Times* describing it as 'barely recognizable as a human body part' in 2007, following the death of its owner, a New Jersey urologist. It was passed to his daughter, who has been offered $100,000 for it but is yet to sell.

DERVORGILLA MATER IOHANNIS BALLIOL SCOTORUM
REGIS FUNDATRIX COLLEGII BALLIOLENSIS

fashioned into jewellery – Charles Dickens
even had the paw of his beloved cat Bob made
into a letter opener. But the heart was special.
An early example is the story behind the red
stone ruin of Sweetheart Abbey, near Dumfries,
Scotland, founded by the renowned beauty
Dervorguilla of Galloway *c.*1210-90, in memory
of her husband John de Balliol (1208-68), who

A seventeenth-century portrait of Dervorguilla of
Galloway, holding the arms of the Earldoms of
Huntingdon and Chester, which she inherited.

co-founded Balliol College, Oxford, with her.
After his death a distraught Dervorguilla had
his heart embalmed and encased in a silver
and ivory casket. She kept this 'silent, sweet

companion' with her until her own death in 1290, aged eighty-one. She was buried in the monastery, which the Cistercian monks came to call Sweetheart Abbey. The effigy of her tomb shows her clasping her husband's heart to her chest for all eternity.

Perhaps the most famous example though is the heart of Percy Bysshe Shelley, who drowned on 8 July 1822 at the age of twenty-nine after his boat *Don Juan* was swallowed by a storm off the north-western coast of Italy. His body was temporarily buried on a beach in Viareggio, but his friends Byron, Leigh Hunt and Captain Edward John Trelawny disinterred the body to cremate it at the same spot. 'The fire was so fierce as to produce a white heat on the iron,' wrote Trelawny, 'and

to reduce its contents to grey ashes. The only portions that were not consumed were some fragments of bones, the jaw, and the skull, but what surprised us all was that the heart remained entire. In snatching this relic from the fiery furnace my hand was severely burnt.'

Regardless of whether or not the fire-resistant object was indeed the heart (the *New York Times* suggested in 1885 that it might have been Shelley's liver soaked in sea water), Mary Shelley kept the heart with her for the rest of her life. In 1852, a year after her death, her son Percy Florence Shelley found the heart in her desk drawer, wrapped in a manuscript of one of her last poems. Only after Percy's death was the heart finally laid to rest, in the family vault at St Peter's Church, Boscombe.

A 'cist' containing a human heart, discovered in the crypt of Christ Church in the city of Cork, Ireland, and acquired by General Pitt Rivers in the 1860s.

The King, the Snuff Box and the Secret Sex Society (1822)

The story attached to this elegant silver snuff box dates to 1822, when King George IV (1762-1830) was conducting a tour of Scotland, the first time an English monarch had visited the country since Charles II's Scottish Coronation in 1651. According to the note inside the object, which is today in the collection of the University of St Andrews, Scotland, it was presented by George while he was in Edinburgh to members of a secret society and sex club known as 'The Most Ancient and Most Puissant Order of the Beggar's Benison and Merryland, Anstruther', known simply as 'The Beggar's Benison'. The gift was thought apt by George – who was notorious for his scandalous profligacy and mistress-taking – because of its contents: a tuft of pubic hair of his lover. 'Hairs from the Mons Veneris of a Royal Courtesan of George IV', reads the note. 'His Majesty was introduced to the Sovereign and Knights of the B.B when he visited Scotland and arrived at the [harbour] of Leith for the first and last time.'

The secret society of the Beggar's Benison would have been delighted with the gift – their mascot was said to be a wig knitted from the pubic hair of the mistresses of King Charles II (alas only the empty wig box survives today). Founded in 1732 in the Scottish fishing village of Anstruther, the club's ranks were filled by men from the highest levels of Scottish society, who gathered in the evenings to drink from phallic vessels known as 'prick glasses', dining, singing bawdy songs, poring over pornography and discussing sex. Nude 'posture molls' were brought in for the

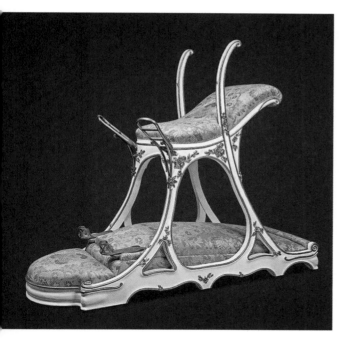

Left: On the subject of the love items of corpulent male British monarchs, special mention should be made of this custom crafted siège d'amour (love chair). *It was built for Edward VII (1841-1910), son of Queen Victoria (1819-1901), by the French furniture maker Soubrier, to allow 'Dirty Bertie', as he was known, to comfortably have sex with two women simultaneously when visiting Le Chabanais brothel in Paris. Exactly how the participants were positioned on/in the contraption remains open to debate.*

Below: A Georgian pornographic painting set in a case, designed to be concealed in a pocket.

members to ogle, striking limber poses on tables to reveal 'the secrets of nature'. Then, the club president would pull out a wooden case, remove a mannequin's head wearing the aforementioned pubic-hair-stitched wig, and in club tradition would parade around the room wearing it on his head as the members cheered.

One ritual for initiation into the club, which was active until 1836, involved all the members cheerfully masturbating together. Club records document the rest of the process, in which the new member was 'prepared' by various assistants in 'a closet, by causing him to propel his Penis until full erection. When thus ready he was escorted with four puffs of the Breath-Horn before the Brethren or Knighthood, and was ordered by the Sovereign to place his Genitals upon the Testing Platter, which was covered with a folded white napkin. The Members and Knights two and two came round in a state of erection and touched the Novice Penis to Penis. Thereafter the special Glass, with the Society's Insignia thereon and Medal attached, was filled with Port Wine, when the new Brother's

health was heartily and humorously drunk, he was told to select an amorous Passage from the Song of Solomon and to read it aloud.'

As well as Edinburgh, there existed a chapter of the society in Manchester, and there were plans for a chapter in St Petersburg, Russia, too, though it's not known whether this ever came to fruition.

Sarah Goodridge's Beauty Revealed *(1828)*

Even to modern viewers this work of the miniaturist's art is a startling sight, and so one can only imagine the reaction of a viewer in its original conservative era. But there never was a grand exhibition because in examining this work we are intruding on the most hidden of secret intimacies. This miniature, a self-portrait, was created solely for an audience of one.

The American miniaturist Sarah Goodridge (1788-1853) was an unmarried woman in her early thirties when she first met Daniel Webster, a married lawyer six years her senior who was making waves as a rising political talent in Massachusetts. Goodridge painted portraits of several members of the Webster family, but from the first sitting with Daniel

an intimacy formed, as is common between artist and subject, that turned into a lifelong friendship of probably more romantic emotion, though there is no specific reference in evidence that confirms this between the two.

By the late 1820s, both Goodridge and Webster were enjoying successful careers. Webster was elected to serve in the United States Senate in

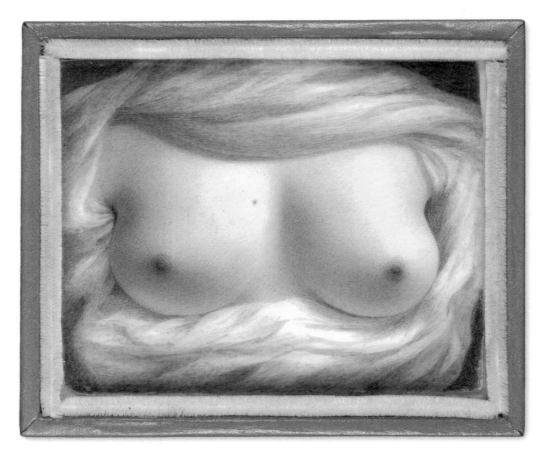

1827, while Goodridge's
characteristic skill with
realism saw her becoming
one of Boston's leading
miniaturists, completing
two commissions a week
and earning enough to
comfortably support her
family. Webster helped
Goodridge find a studio
and rooms and years
later Goodridge would
be in a position to
return the favour by
loaning Webster several
thousand dollars.

The two maintained
decades of correspondence,
of which only forty
carefully worded letters
from Webster survive
(there are none to be found
by Goodridge). The tone
is cordial, and the subjects
discussed are quotidian,
and in the earliest letter
Webster thanks Goodridge
for her 'kind wishes' for

Daniel Webster, in a miniature portrait painted by
Sarah Goodridge in 1827.

Mrs Webster's health. All is conducted with
meticulous propriety, but there is a poignancy
to how, as the correspondence progresses, his
salutations gradually change from 'Madam'
to 'Dear Madam' to 'Dear Miss G.' and finally
'My dear, good friend'.

Goodridge left her Boston home only
twice, each time for a journey to Washington
in the winters of 1828 and 1841 – the first, it
is thought, to console Webster on the recent
passing of his first wife; and then again after he
had separated from his second wife. According
to an inscription on a backing paper, now
lost, to the miniature artwork shown here,
Goodridge gave it to Webster during her visit

of 1828. According to Webster's descendants,
she had created it specially for him.

Beauty Revealed, as this piece is titled, is a
self-portrait painted on a slice of ivory so thin
as to be translucent, measuring just 6.7 × 8 cm
(2⅝ × 3⅛ in). The giving of any miniature, let
alone one with the subject matter of Goodridge's
gift, was a deeply personal move reserved only
for lovers or close family. Examining one is an
act of intimacy in itself, as one has to bring it
close to the face to examine its details, and they
were often worn pinned to the breast for

closeness to the heart and the body. Though Goodridge's painting omits her face, the carefully drawn mole presents a clue to her identity that only a lover could read. Nude art in America was a rarity at this time, and while miniatures of lovers' body parts like eyes had existed (see pages 158-9), Goodridge's breasts were a radical innovation.

Senator Webster accepted Goodridge's gift, which would be passed down in the Webster

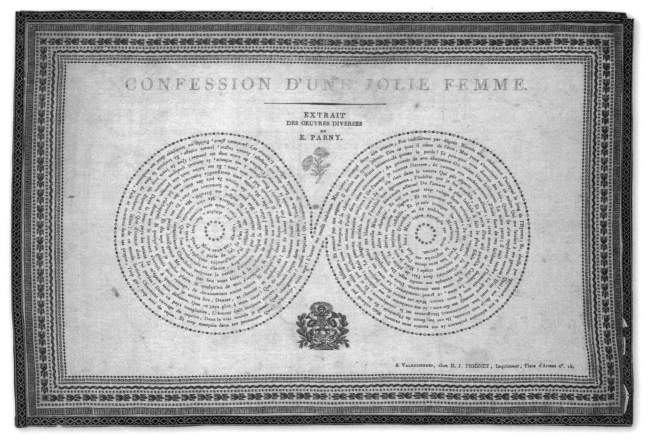

CONFESSION D'UNE JOLIE FEMME.

EXTRAIT
DES OEUVRES DIVERSES
DE
E. PARNY.

A VALENCIENNES, chez H. J. PRIGNET, Imprimeur, Place d'Armes n°. 16,

family along with her easel and paintbox, and Goodridge painted Webster's portrait at least twelve times over two decades. But the two never married, and she lived her entire life in the Boston area, with her portraiture business providing enough income to raise an orphaned niece and look after her infirm mother for eleven years. By 1850 her eyesight was failing, and she retired to a house in Reading, Massachusetts, where three years later she suffered a stroke and died at the age of sixty-five.

Above: A silk handkerchief of 1802 elaborately printed with extracts of the erotic writings of Evariste Désiré de Forges, Chevalier (and later) Vicomte de Parny (1753-1814) in the shape of breasts, with asterisks forming the nipples. Titled Confession d'une jolie femme (Confession of a Beautiful Woman), *the scandalous pocket pornography could be hidden on one's person (until an absent-minded nose-blow in public ruined the subterfuge).*

Opposite: Between about 1820 and 1845, Sarah Goodridge made at least four self-portraits, varying significantly in composition and pose. This miniature self-portrait dates to 1830, and measures just 9.52 × 6.73cm (3¾ × 2⅜ in).

Note from the Bank of Love (1847)
A Brief History of Valentine's Day

What, one wonders, would a freshly resurrected Saint Valentine of the third century make of the celebratory customs and commercial paraphernalia surrounding his feast day of 14 February in the twenty-first century? Somehow it isn't difficult to imagine the man swiftly begging to be returned to the grave. Or perhaps he'd be *thrilled* to learn of the Valentine's Day '18+ Adults Meal' offered by Burger King Israel in 2017, which accompanied the fast food with a blindfold, an adult toy and a miniature feather duster. Or the pill sold by French inventor Christian Poincheval in 2015 for lovers to take on Valentine's Day so that their flatulence would smell of ginger and not ruin the date; or the champagne-flavoured Marmite spread released especially for Valentine's Day 2008.

Saint Valentine's confoundment would be understandable given the fact that the modern romantic nature of the celebration has nothing to do with the original feast day. We would also have to settle on *which* Saint Valentine to

A 'skit note' (a satirical, political or fantasy banknote) piece of currency from the 'Bank of Love', to be given as a valentine, dated 14 February 1847 and signed by Cupid. 'Promise to pay to you on Demand the entire LOVE of the suppliant who sends this.'

inflict this indignity on – early hagiographies
associate three men of the third century
with the name: one Roman, one of Terni
(central Italy), and a mention of a third man
who suffered in a Roman province in Africa,
although nothing else is written of him.
According to the *Oxford Dictionary of the
Christian Church* (1983), each of these stories
can be whittled down to 'a common nucleus
of fact' and they may actually refer to a
single person. Trying to sieve facts from
hagiographies is like trying to pin smoke
to a cork board, especially as they become

*The flower-crowned skull alleged to be that of Saint
Valentine, in the church of Santa Maria in Cosmedin,
Rome, Italy.*

increasingly romanticised over the centuries,
but the prevailing understanding is that Saint
Valentine was a member of the clergy, either a
priest or a bishop, of the Roman Empire, who
ministered to persecuted Christians. He was
imprisoned in Rome, and according to one
early tradition restored the sight of Julia, the
blind daughter of his jailer Asterius, who with
his extended family subsequently came to believe

in Jesus and were all baptised. Saint Valentine was martyred in Rome, and his body buried at a Christian cemetery on the Via Flaminia on 14 February, which since at least the eighth century has been observed as the Feast of Saint Valentine. Today he's also recognised as the patron saint of asthma and beekeepers.

So far, so unromantic. The love association came much later, with the work of Geoffrey Chaucer. As we've seen previously, medieval manuscripts were full of romantic advice,[1] but it was Chaucer who made the first link between budding romance and Saint Valentine's feast day of 14 February. In his poem *Parlement of Foules* (1382), which was written to celebrate the anniversary of the engagement of King Richard II to Anne of Bohemia, he writes the earliest of valentines, linking the mating season of birds (and by implication, through the use of nature as a mirror of Creation, the desires of man also) at this time of year. The whole 'parliament of fowls' gathers in the Garden of Love: 'For this was on seynt Valentynes day, When every foul comyth there to chese his make' ('For this

was on Saint Valentine's day, When every bird came there to choose his mate').

In fact 14 February was a little too early for the avian mating season in fourteenth-century England, but no matter, the symbolism was established. In the *Charter of the Court of Love* (1400) of Charles VI of France we find the earliest mention of a love-themed celebration on 14 February at Mantes-la-Jolie, where a festival of love songs and poetry, jousts and dances was held, and during which a special event was arranged for ladies of the court to hear and rule on disputes between lovers.[2]

The earliest known valentine was written in this same century, a rondeau by Charles, Duke of Orléans, for his wife while he was

---

[2] In the same century, England had the grand event known as the Loveday of 1458, but this was of an entirely different nature – in this context 'love' means 'agreement'. Loveday was designed to be a symbolic reconciliation between the warring English factions of York and Lancaster, to prevent civil war. Peace was established by the Loveday, but not for long. Within a few months skirmishes were breaking out and until that same year the enemies faced off at the Battle of Blore Heath.

Opposite: A 'Vinegar Valentine', sent on Valentine's Day to hated persons.

Below: Margery Brewes' 1477 letter to her fiancé John Paston, the earliest valentine written in English.

---

[1] They even provided gift ideas – Andreas Capellanus of the twelfth century, for example, in his *Art of Courtly Love*, recommends buying one's partner the romantic gift of a washbasin.

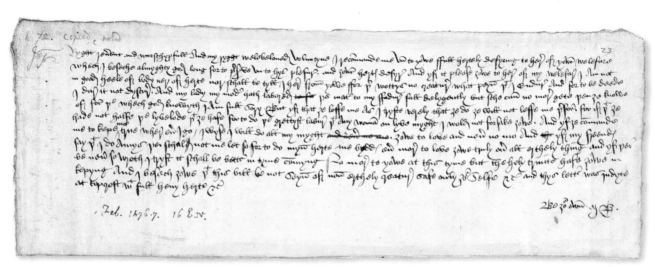

HEART-AGONY IS A FREQUENT AFFLICTION WITH YOU.

Into your soft and susceptible heart,
Cupid, sly Cupid sends many a dart!
Some arrow-proof armor you ought to procure;
Then the pangs of these wounds you'd not have to endure.

imprisoned in the Tower of London following his capture at the Battle of Agincourt in 1415. 'I am already sick of love, My very gentle Valentine,' it begins. 'Since for me you were born too soon, And I for you was born too late.' The earliest surviving valentine in English is written by a woman to her future husband. In the collection of correspondence known as the Paston letters of 1477, Margery Brewes addresses John Paston as 'my right well-beloved Valentine' and worries that she is 'not in good health of body nor of heart, nor shall I be till I hear from you'. She tells how her mother has so far failed to persuade her father to increase her dowry; 'but if you love me,' she writes, 'as I trust verily that you do, you will not leave me therefore.' The couple went on to marry.

By the eighteenth century in England, Valentine's Day had become an established occasion for couples to gift each other flowers and sweets, and send cards with verses and illustrations produced by printers known as 'mechanical valentines'. Male suitors struggling to find inspiration were able to consult guides like *The Complete Valentine Writer: or, the Young Men and Maidens' Best Assistant* of 1780 with its suggested verses. Into the nineteenth century and paper valentines were now so popular to send on 14 February that factories were churning them out on an industrial scale. When the cost of postage plummeted with the introduction of the postage stamp in 1840, the number of valentines flying through the postal system rocketed to 400,000, up from 6,000 in 1835.

It was also now easy to send valentine cards anonymously, which led to the curious Victorian phenomenon of the 'Vinegar Valentine', opposite in spirit to the traditional valentine in that they were sarcastic and vindictive notes that would be sent to a person one hated. Essentially, it was an early form of trolling. Young women unlucky in love

were sent drawings of elderly spinsters with rhyming captions like 'old maid – She's caught a poor cat and a bird, but she can't snare a man, so we've heard. It's the old maid's fate to lose out on a mate'. A young male country bumpkin might receive a similar caustic cartoon captioned 'good-for-nothing farmer – You stupid lazy fellow, you think you are quite frisky, The only corn you've knowledge of is that made into whisky.' 'Hi Sourpuss!' reads another. 'Your scowl must give folks ulcers. Who could love you but your mother? We know that you aren't two-faced … If you were you'd wear the other!'

Today Valentine's Day is observed around the world. In Afghanistan, in the time before the Taliban, Koch-e-Gul-Faroushi (Flower Street) in downtown Kabul would be covered in flower arrangements on Valentine's Day; while in India, the suppression of public expression of affection, common in antiquity with the worship of Kamadeva (see page 25), began to loosen in the early 1990s, and Valentine's Day began to be celebrated with the influence of television channels like MTV. In Japan and indeed other Asian countries including South Korea, Valentine's Day involves women giving presents to men to express their love, and then a month later, on 14 March, occurs 'White Day', when the man has to give a present worth three times as much. (In Taiwan it is the reverse, with males buying the gifts on Valentine's Day.)

Not everyone is thrilled at the prospect of a day for couples to openly celebrate their romantic good fortune. In Japan, the Revolutionary Alliance of Unpopular Men was founded in 2006 by a group of unhappy singletons who march through the streets every year in anti-love protest, claiming to provide 'a mental safety net for people all over the world who aren't popular', with their goal being to 'overthrow love capitalism' and

'build a brighter future for the unpopular'. (Their 2018 protest was a bit of a damp squib, however, as they neglected to arrange the correct public permit and were forced to protest among themselves indoors.) 'Although they invited other like-minded people to join them in their protest before the event took place,' reported *Japan Today* at the 2021

The Revolutionary Alliance of Unpopular Men conduct their 'Smash Valentine's Day' protest as they march through the streets of Shibuya district in Tokyo, Japan on 14 February 2015.

protest, 'only a dozen or so people ended up protesting, with the members looking very similar to those from previous years.'

The Unexpected Origins
of the Love Song

The first face you picture when listening to a power ballad might not be that of an irascible Victorian naturalist, but the fact is that Charles Darwin was the first to link animal song and courtship, to much controversy at the time.[1] Why do we sing of love? Devoting considerable time to studying the phenomenon of song in *In the Descent of Man* (1871), Darwin claimed that to find the origin of music one need only study the melodies of birdsong and recognise their importance in attracting the opposite sex. Therefore, the same could be true of 'primeval man, or rather some early progenitor of man, [who] probably first used his voice in producing true musical cadences … This power would have been especially exerted during the courtship of the sexes, would have expressed various emotions, such as love, jealousy, triumph, and would have served as a challenge to rivals.' All song, then, originates with the love song. This power we continue to find in the modern singer: 'The impassioned orator, bard, or musician, when with his varied tones and cadences he excites the strongest emotions in his hearers, little suspects that he uses the same means by which his half-human ancestors long ago aroused each other's ardent passions, during their courtship and rivalry … Music … awakens the gentler feelings of tenderness and love, which readily pass into devotion … love is still the commonest theme of our songs.'

Recent research in genetics studies continue to reinforce Darwin's musical theories – at least with birds. One study conducted by Sarah Earp and Donna L. Maney at Emory University in 2012 showed that the neural patterns of female songbirds listening to the mating songs of males show a similar neural 'pleasure-reward' response to those of humans enjoying a great musical performance. It was also recently found that in sparrows the 'monogamy hormone' vasotocin is boosted by the singing of male sparrows. Nightingales can possess a repertoire of hundreds of songs; the ornithologists Donald E. Kroodsma and Linda

D. Parker have written about a brown thrasher that appeared to have a repertoire of more than 1,800. Survival of the fittest, then, could also be said to be the survival of the most melodic.

When it comes to primates – humans aside – there is much less evidence of romantic song. Mainly because apes don't really sing. This was once confirmed by Leonard Williams, father of musician John Williams, who spent years living with a community of woolly monkeys after setting up a sanctuary at Murrayton House in the Cornish countryside. Williams stated authoritatively from his years of listening to them having sex that there was no discernible

---

1 Incidentally, even Darwin didn't like to picture his own face. Aghast at seeing a photographic portrait of himself in 1855, he wrote to Joseph Hooker: 'If I really have as bad an expression, as my photograph gives me, how I can have one single friend is surprising.'

Opposite: Song of Songs (1923), a painting by Egon Tschirch inspired by Solomon's erotic Song of Songs in the Bible.

The cuneiform tablet bearing The Love Song for Shu-Sin, *on display at the Istanbul Museum of the Ancient Orient.*

form of song, merely 'sighs, sobs, grunts and squeaks, [that] are anything but musical'. For the earliest recorded human love song, we can go back at least as far as the verse of the Song of Songs in the Old Testament, dated to the sixth to third centuries BC, which for the longest time was considered the oldest love song in existence. That was, until the archaeologist Austen Henry Layerd excavated the site of Nineveh in 1846-7 and discovered the library of the Assyrian king Ashurbanipal. One of the cuneiform tablets recovered there contained The Love Song for Shu-Sin, which was composed *c*.2000 BC. Its content wasn't

actually recognised until 1951, when it was translated by the Sumerologist Samuel Noah Kramer, who wrote: 'I soon realised that I was reading a poem, divided into a number of stanzas, which celebrated beauty and love, a joyous bride and a king named Shu-Sin (who ruled over the land of Sumer close to four thousand years ago). As I read it again and yet again, there was no mistaking its content. What I held in my hand was one of the oldest love songs written down by the hand of man.' It was not just a song, but a recitation as part of a sacred annual rite in which the king would symbolically marry the goddess of love and procreation, Inanna. In consummating their marriage, fertility and prosperity would be assured for the coming year. The opening verses from Kramer's translation:

Bridegroom, dear to my heart,
Goodly is your beauty, honeysweet,
Lion, dear to my heart,
Goodly is your beauty, honeysweet.

You have captivated me, let me stand
*   tremblingly before you.*
Bridegroom, I would be taken by you
*   to the bedchamber,*
You have captivated me, let me stand
*   tremblingly before you.*
Lion, I would be taken by you to the
*   bedchamber.*

Though usurped by *The Love Song for Shu-Sin* for the crown of oldest love song, Song of Songs in the Old Testament is still a fascinatingly strange text, with meanings and questions debated by scholars to this day, such as how so much explicit eroticism made it into the Bible? The book is attributed to King Solomon for the wisdom it espouses, yet uniquely for a biblical book it focuses not on law, nor Covenant, nor the God of Israel, nor the kind of teachings of Proverbs or Ecclesiastes. Instead, it celebrates sexual love:

How beautiful your sandalled feet, O prince's daughter! Your graceful legs are like jewels, the work of a craftsman's hands. Your navel is a rounded goblet that never lacks blended wine. Your waist is a mound of wheat encircled by lilies. Your breasts are like two fawns, twins of a gazelle ... How beautiful and pleasant you are, O loved one, with all your delights! Your stature is like a palm tree, and your breasts are like its clusters. I say I will climb the palm tree and lay hold of its fruit. Oh may your breasts be like clusters of the vine, and the scent of your breath like apples, and your mouth like the best wine. (Song of Songs 7:1–3, 6–9)

Some have interpreted the intense passion of the erotic language as being metaphorical for God's love for his faithful, which it may well be, though the image of Him metaphorically climbing his naked followers like a palm tree to grab their fruit doesn't seem to make it into many Sunday sermons.

In both ancient Greece and Rome, male singers that sang of love often did so from the woman's perspective and in feminine vocal styles, none of which sat well with older men who wanted a more masculine energy radiated from their national culture. The Roman educator Quintilian (AD*c*.35-*c*.100), for example, complains about the contemporary music of the early Roman Imperial era, grumbling that songs had been 'emasculated by the lascivious melodies of our effeminate stage'. These girly pop hits 'no doubt destroyed such manly vigour as we still possess'. Seneca the Elder (*c*.54 BC-AD*c*.39) had made the same complaint, outraged that 'the revolting pursuits of singing and dancing have these effeminates in their power, braiding their hair

and thinning their voices to a feminine lilt ... This is the model our young men have!'[1]

In ancient Greece the lyric tradition went back to Sappho (*c*.630-*c*.570 BC), from Eresos or Mytilene on the island of Lesbos, known for her brilliant lyric poetry, which she wrote to be sung while accompanied by musical instruments like the cithara (an early guitar). The elegant simplicity of Sappho's lyrics renders them timeless, and radio-friendly even today. *Love Shook my Heart*, for example:

---

1 This kind of complaint can be found later in the Islamic world as well, where mukhannathun ('effeminate ones') singers were popular. Legend tells of a noble singer of the older traditional style berating his son for adopting the mukhannathun style, yelling, 'Be quiet, ignorant boy!' The son replies that the father has lived in poverty for sixty years from singing in the old style, while the son has already earned more money than the old man has ever seen by singing in the new style.

Musicians performing a love song, from the collection of love lyrics known as the Codex Manesse.

'Love shook my heart / Like the wind on the mountain / Troubling the oak-trees.' Male singers adapted the style while attempting to butch up the content, though were forced to recognise what made it work so well. Pindar of Thebes (c.518–c.438 BC), who of the nine lyric poets was praised by Quintilian as the greatest, sang of worthy men, but was also forced unhappily to admit that in his approach, 'I must think maidenly thoughts. And utter them with my tongue.'

Today the distant origins of the modern love song in Europe are traditionally traced back to early Christian notions of love celebrated in poetry and hymn, along with the competing tradition that arose of songs of courtly love originating in the medieval era, of the kind sung by travelling bards telling tales of knights rescuing fair maidens. Only recently has an alternative, deeper influence been theorised, by the musical historian Ted Gioia, who points to the cultural influences that came with the invasions of Europe by the Islamic Empire. Among the new traditions and rich scholastic resources pouring in were the love songs of the elite singing women known as *qiyān*. These were highly trained female entertainers and skilful singers, most of whom were enslaved, brought from the Middle East to Europe. Here in the songs of enslaved women singing adoring love songs of their masters and members of nobility we find the ethos of courtly love before courtly love existed in its recognised form, and troubadours a staple in court entertainment. Indeed, much of the work that survives today of medieval Arabic female poets is the work of *qiyān*, an oft forgotten group of extraordinary women.

The Courting Manuscript of Henry Hilditch Bulkeley-Johnson (c.1870)

These are pages of an extraordinary illustrated manuscript, written and drawn *c.*1870 by a middle-aged English hops merchant named Henry Hilditch Bulkeley-Johnson (1825-90), as part of his romantic campaign to win the hand of a wealthy Irish divorcée, Emma Fielding Leet (called 'Zöe' in the text). The allegorical story, told by the Victorian amateur-Dante in cantos of iambic pentameter, along with fifty full-page illustrations and detailed borders, tells of a bull chasing the couple through a magical Irish countryside. The bull was a common allegorical symbol of England, but it is also an animal that features prominently in Bulkeley-Johnson's family coat of arms.

As the pair are chased by the animal through the landscape, inspired by the abandoned and reputedly haunted estate of Loftus Hall in Wexford, Bulkeley-Johnson flexes his knowledge of nature, history and architecture and his skills as a graphic artist. Fairies, banshees and ghosts are encountered by the pair until gradually the story becomes a more serious critical commentary on Anglo-Irish relations of the time:

How thy woes and thy sins, thy despair
  and distress,
May be traced to one source: legislation of ours!
Britannia's ill use of her infinite powers!
She chases oppression from shore on to shore,
But closes her eye to the tyrannous sore,
Which rules in its might, as it broods at
  her door,
O! Herald the man! Who shall settle the day,
When Britain's reproach shall be all swept
  away …

This leads to a climax of four full-page dramatic scenes of 'Sowing ye winds of injustice' as the British carry out an eviction; 'Reaping the whirlwind of revolution' in a scene of troops fighting

Irishmen; 'The harvest home of ruin' as a church is shown abandoned; and 'Seeking a better life' written over an emigration scene.

Both Henry and Emma had been married before. There is no record of what happened to Henry's first wife, Sarah, but Emma successfully divorced her first husband, a brewer named William Bowden Wetherman, in 1869 on the grounds of adultery, after he ran off with a woman named Keziah Mealing. A year later, Henry presented her with his gift of the manuscript, which clearly went down well – the two married in Dublin in 1871 and lived the rest of their lives together in London.

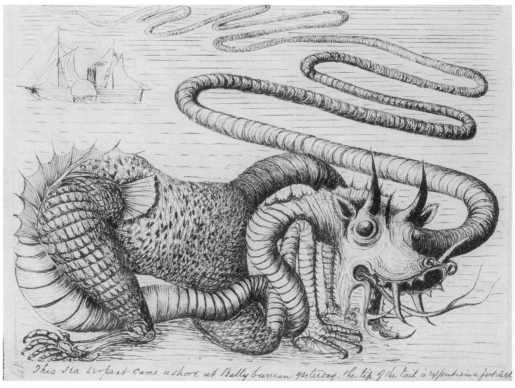

This sea serpent came ashore at Ballybunnian yesterday, the tip of the tail is expected in a fortnight

I first thought of Joe, whose fond agitation,
Made me fear for her fate in the dread situation.

I pictured the Bull in her cage having caught her,
And worked in her savage attention of slaughter,
Saw Joe laid prostrate before my own eyes,
An innocent victim to brute sacrifice —
I thought of her mangled in blood and in gore
Companion twin sister, my Joe no more —
I fancied the anguish and sorrowing thru
I carried the tidings which stood Eversden:
The sad desolation which sat brooding there;
The woe and the weeping in grief and despair:
The father's distraction, his tears flowing wild,
The comfort refused for the loss of his child —
Vain efforts to minister any relief —
My parting, and leaving them all in their grief:
The worm which would gnaw to be satisfied never,
And the scene which would hang up before me for ever

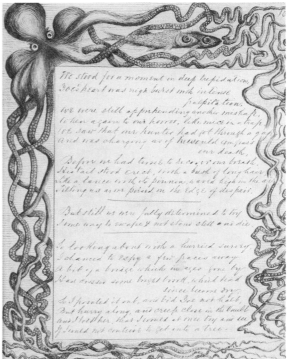

We stood for a moment in deep trepidation,
Joe's heart was nigh burst with intense
                              palpitation.

We were still apprehending another mishap,
When again to our horror, like mice in a trap,
We saw that our hunter had got through a gap,
And was charging as if he would compass
                              our death.
Before we had time to recover our breath.
His tail stood erect, with a bush of long hair,
Like a lance with its pennon, waved high in the air
Telling us as we poised on the edge of despair.

But still we were fully determined to try
Some way to escape & not stand still & die.

So looking about with a hurried survey
I chanced to espy a few paces away
A bit of a bridge which in ages gone by
Had crossed some bright brook which had
                              since become dry.
So I pointed it out, and bid Joe not halt,
But hurry along, and creep close in the vault
And told her that seemed it me try and see
If I could not contrive to get into a tree.

THE POWER OF GENTLENESS.

THE HARVEST HOME OF RUIN

So, onward we strolled
What a pity! we did

Victorian Cryptic Postcards and the Flower Code

How to secretly communicate intimate feelings in a time before the technology of telephone, text message or email? One way was through subtle gesturing with a hand fan. An early mention of the secret 'language of the fan' can be found in a 1740 issue of *The Gentleman's Magazine*, which reveals that a woman touching the tip of the fan with a finger meant 'I wish to speak to you', twirling the fan warned 'We are watched', drawing it across the cheek signalled 'I love you', while holding the fan in the right hand in front of the face meant 'Follow me'. In eighteenth-century New England, couples solved the problem of having intimate conversations in privacy by using the six-foot-long courting stick, a hollow tube through which one could whisper sweet nothings out of earshot, while keeping a respectful distance. Thomas Edison, who had used Morse code since the age of fifteen when he worked as a telegraph operator, taught the code to his second wife, Mina Miller, so that the two could display their affection to each other secretly when in company. Edison even proposed in Morse code and nicknamed his two children Dot and Dash.[1]

1 Telegrams, dictated to operators like a young Edison, offered less privacy, but sometimes immediacy was more important. When John Sholto Douglas, 9th Marquess of Queensberry (1844-1900), heard about his son Alfred's intimate relationship with Oscar Wilde, he sent his son a blistering letter on 1 April 1894 ordering him to cease or face disownment, signing it 'your disgusted, so-called father, Queensberry'. Alfred replied with the telegram: 'What a funny little man you are.'

For those wanting to send letters that were at risk of being read by overprotective parents and busybodies, the solution was found in code-writing. Sending cryptic postcards by using basic substitution cyphers was a fashion of young lovers in the nineteenth and early twentieth centuries wanting to conduct their romance in secret. Today these cards, with their glimpses into illicit affairs, are extremely rare and highly sought after by collectors. Featured here is a selection of cryptic lovers' postcards kindly provided for this book by the German hacker and IT security expert Tobias Schrödel, from his collection of 235 such items. 'It is not the picture that makes a postcard special, it is the text,' he says. 'Every single piece has a story to tell. Sometimes you read about an ancient life hidden "behind the curtains" due to social boundaries.'

Opposite: An American couple use a courting stick, to have an intimate conversation with privacy.

Below: Dated 23 March 1882, this postcard sent from Freiburg, Germany, to Lausanne, Switzerland, is a carefully written-out cipher that hides an eyebrow-raisingly erotic message. A sample extract: 'I love you and I long to be able to intoxicate my heart with yours to push my love into your love Oh it makes me feel so good to write to you slowly it frees my heart from wild longing Oh if only I could press my face into your lap your hands kissing my hot cheeks kissing your feet in which my head rests looking up to you with your longing almighty gaze kiss my hot cheeks kiss your feet in which my head rests look up to you with your longing almighty look of love of longing bend down sweet love that I press my lips into your mouth that my arms embrace you …'

Above: On 1 February 1901 the Kiel-based author of this card wrote their monthly card to a lover in Zeitz: 'My dearest sweetheart bride, I am very sorry that I lost my January card, I have searched almost all the shops here in Kiel unfortunately without success. January ends just as it began, very cold this morning it was 12 degrees yesterday, it was still the most beautiful snow weather with 2 degrees. But this, my soulmate darling shall not cool our hearts flaming with true loyal love, the hotter however the sweet kisses shall burn … My dear child how did my last visit go for you? Very good for me, I still taste the small sweet kisses…'

Right: This citizen of Zemun (an Austro-Hungarian municipality now a part of modern Belgrade), tries to excuse his cheating by blaming his (ex?) girlfriend of doing it first: 'Paula, sweetie, do you have a heart? So save me, because in a few days I will perish. You know that out of desperation I fell into the hands of a reckless female cashier. If you had remained faithful to me I would not have become so lost myself. A kiss from your Andre.'

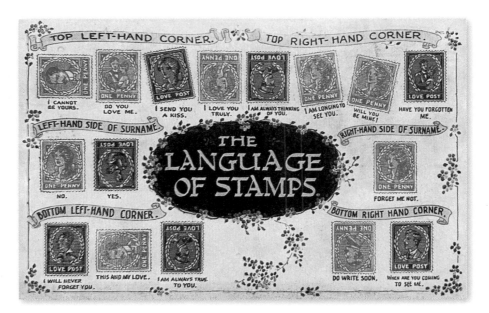

The 'language of stamps'. Stamp positions and their meanings:

TOP LEFT-HAND CORNER.
- I CANNOT BE YOURS.
- DO YOU LOVE ME.
- I SEND YOU A KISS.

TOP RIGHT-HAND CORNER.
- I LOVE YOU TRULY.
- I AM ALWAYS THINKING OF YOU.
- I AM LONGING TO SEE YOU.
- WILL YOU BE MINE?
- HAVE YOU FORGOTTEN ME.

THE LANGUAGE OF STAMPS

LEFT-HAND SIDE OF SURNAME.
- NO.
- YES.

RIGHT-HAND SIDE OF SURNAME.
- FORGET ME NOT.

BOTTOM LEFT-HAND CORNER.
- I WILL NEVER FORGET YOU.
- THIS AND MY LOVE.
- I AM ALWAYS TRUE TO YOU.

BOTTOM RIGHT HAND CORNER.
- DO WRITE SOON.
- WHEN ARE YOU COMING TO SEE ME.

Above: The 'language of stamps', i.e., applying the stamp to the envelope in a particular way to convey meaning, developed in the early 1900s across Europe, although the code varied between languages. This helped young courting couples bypass the scrutiny of parents who might read their mail.

Below: A scandal of Mansfeld, Germany in 1902. Lucie, the daughter of the Earl of Mansfeld, conducts an illicit affair through cryptic postcards with the son of the bookseller in the nearby village of Eisleben. On 5 September 1902 she writes:
'My dear Paul, hopefully you came home well the day before yesterday. Sunday I will probably go for a walk with my sister. Maybe to Orner. Should you come here, we will pass there at Schiele [a pub?] at half-past-three o'clock. Unfortunately it is raining tonight. Hopefully it will be nice on Sunday. Many warm greetings, my dear Paul, your faithful Lucie. See you again soon.'

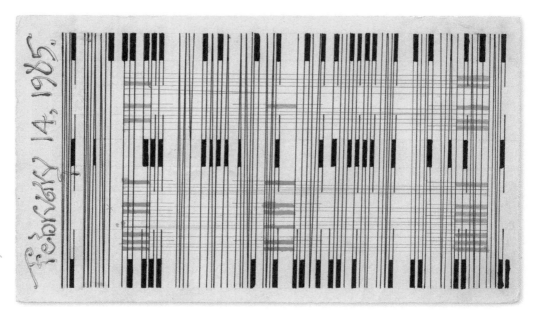

Above: A card sent between two inhabitants of Stirling, USA, on 14 February 1905. Not strictly cryptic, but an anamorphic hidden message. Tilt the card away from you until the tall letters become shorter and legible, and you find the Valentine's Day message: 'We want to see / my papa and me / love superfine our valentine / because we love you.'

Right: The cover of a 1901 German guide to secret writing for lovers, The Most Secure Protection of the Secrecy of Letters – an absolutely secure secret writing for lovers and friends, businessmen and politicians. Cannot be deciphered by unauthorised persons. By Emil Katz.

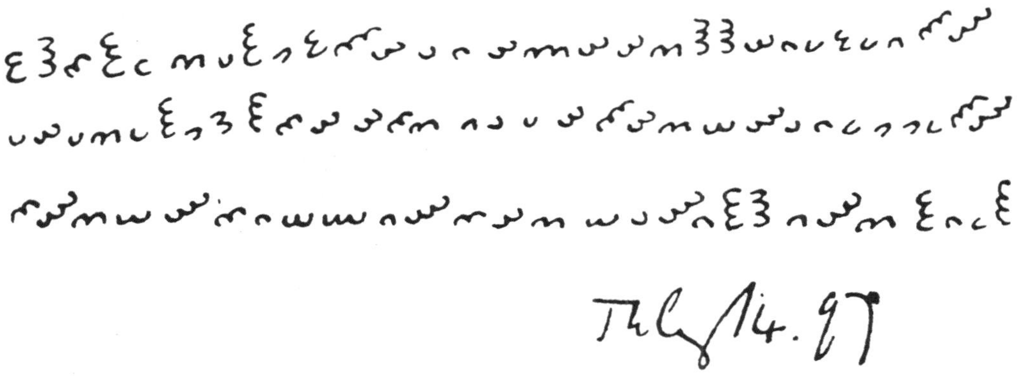

(The Dorabella cypher — a sequence of handwritten semicircle symbols — appears at the top of the page, followed by a handwritten inscription reading "14. 97".)

Above: The unsolved 'Dorabella cypher', written by the married composer Edward Elgar in 1897 to a family friend seventeen years his junior, Dora Penny. The cypher of the suspected love missive has never been broken – it's possible that it's not even a text but a melody, the eight different positions of the semicircles, rotating clockwise, matching the notes of the scale. Confident claims of cracking the code have been made but none has gained consensus of success, and often provide a message even more nonsensical – see that of Tim S. Roberts of Central Queensland University, for example: 'P.S. Now droop beige weeds set in it – pure idiocy – one entire bed! Luigi Ccibunud lovingly tuned liuto studio two.'

Below: As well as cryptic writing and the hidden meanings of stamp positioning, Victorian lovers also had floriography, or the language of flowers, at their disposal. Each flower carried a different meaning, allowing complex messages to be conveyed simply with a carefully assembled bouquet.

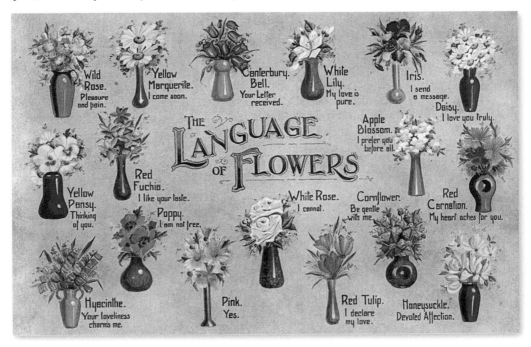

Matches Made in Heaven – The Hot Air Balloon Wedding Craze

A lot of strange things have taken place in the history of hot air balloons. On 16 October 1798, Frenchman Pierre Testu Brissy replaced his balloon's basket with a specially trained horse. The equestrian aeronaut made his ascent astride the animal ('equally calm and undaunted', according to reports) from Bellevue Park in Paris, but they failed to clear the castle wall and collided with a chimney, which tore a hole in the balloon's envelope and down they went. On 3 May 1808, two Frenchmen named de Grandpré and de Pique settled a quarrel over the affections of a dancer named Mademoiselle Tirevit by duelling with pistols from the baskets of two hot air balloons 2,000 feet above Paris. De Grandpré scored a hit that collapsed his rival's balloon and sent it crashing to the rooftops below, killing him. And in the 1920s there developed a craze in the USA and the United Kingdom for the miniature 'hopper' balloons, which like a jetpack could be strapped to the back of a person to allow them to leap high into the air. 'Balloon jumping' became a daredevil sport that disappeared in less than a year thanks to stories illustrating its staggeringly high mortality rate, like that of Aircraftsman 'Brainy' Dobbs of the British Royal Air Force who decided he could leap over an electrified high-tension cable, but, as it fatally turned out, couldn't.

Others had more romantic purposes in mind for the hot air balloon.[1] The earliest documented aerial-wedding proposal was made by the French Socialist Philosopher Claude Henri de Rouvroy, Comte de Saint-Simon. In 1802 news came of the death of the husband of the famed writer Anne Louise Germaine de Staël (1766-1817). The Comte leapt into action: he divorced his wife, sped to Geneva, and arrived breathless at Mme de Staël's door to let her know that he and she were 'the two most extraordinary persons who exist', that they should marry in a hot air balloon and together create a child 'who will startle the world at large'. Mme de Staël closed the door in his face.

The first recorded air wedding took place a few years later, between the young Belgian aeronaut Georges Raoul Thiel, and Madeleine Bailly. A Brussels burgomaster presided over the ceremony in a balloon named *Lune de Miel* ('Honeymoon') as they floated above a public square, before the newlyweds took off across the countryside and landed a few miles away in a cow pasture. Less pleasant was the balloon flight in 1824 of the English aeronaut Thomas Harris, who invited his fiancée to climb the sky

---

1 Just as others again would have for the aeroplane years later. Lawrence Sperry (1892-1923), inventor of the first autopilot system in 1914, married his wife Winifred in 1918 and together they were reported by *Flying Magazine* to be 'the first couple to take an aerial honeymoon' after they flew from Amityville to Governors Island. Interestingly Sperry is also credited with the invention of another aerial tradition: the 'Mile-High Club'. In November 1916 he took the married socialite Dorothy Peirce up in an autopilot-equipped Curtiss Flying Boat, which crash-landed a short time later in water outside of New York. A pair of duck-hunters rowed out to the crash site to help and saw that both Sperry and Peirce were naked. Sperry claimed that the force of the crash had 'divested' them of their clothing.

Opposite: Aerial wedding of Margaret Buckley and Edward T. Davis, 27 September 1888, Rhode Island, USA.

Burrell Photo Artist. 357 WESTMINSTER ST.
1888 Providence. R.I.

Balloon Wedding.—98th Ascension.

with him from Vauxhall, London. At altitude he opened a valve to level off, but the valve would not then close, and the balloon began to sink. The couple desperately threw out the ballast and everything in the basket, including their own clothing, but still they plummeted. Harris finally kissed his fiancée goodbye and jumped to his death – this slowed the descent enough to save her life.

Left: Mary Elizabeth Walsh and Charles M. Colton exchanged vows in the balloon P.T. Barnum *piloted by Washington Donaldson, high above an estimated crowd of 50,000 spectators at the Cincinnati Hippodrome, Ohio, on 19 October 1874.*

Below: On 20 September 1989, Dodo Bolli of Bubikon, Switzerland, set the world record for the longest bridal veil; she left her wedding ceremony by hot air balloon with 55 metres of white material trailing beneath her.

The first American sky wedding went considerably smoother, with *Harper's Weekly* reporting in 1865 of Mary West Jenkins of Northampton, Massachusetts, and her fiancé John F. Boynton taking off from Manhattan's Central Park in a plushly carpeted basket draped with red and gold damask, to the cheers of 6,000 onlookers. High above the city of New York they signed a marriage contract, then landed in the suburbs and rode back into town at night.

The 27 September 1888 wedding of Margaret Buckley and Edward T. Davis at the Rhode Island State Fair, pictured on page 223, was designed to outdo even this event in glamour and scale. The *Illustrated Newspaper* estimated

Construction on the [Hoover] dam continued during this wedding ceremony in a cableway skip dangling over the project on 18 December 1931.

a crowd of 40,000 watched the gigantic balloon *Commonwealth* lift the bridal car of Davis and Buckley into the sky as twenty-four men dropped the guy ropes. The honeymoon got off to a rough start, however, as they were soon forced to crash-land at dusk in a swamp near Easton, Massachusetts, about thirty miles away from their departure point. The wedding party was 'obliged to cling to the ropes above the basket to keep out of the water', before being fished out of the swamp. The couple decided to continue their journey by rail.

Lost in Gold – Gustav Klimt and The Kiss *(1907-8)*

'A kiss is a secret which takes the lips for the ear,' wrote Edmond Rostand in his 1897 play *Cyrano de Bergerac*. Into his painting *The Kiss* (1907-8), Gustav Klimt (1862-1918) pours copious secrets, with his unique technique of working with gold dust and leaf, learned from his father, a goldsmith. It's one of the most famous loving embraces in the history of art; but the longer one gazes at it, the more one notices details hidden amid its avant-garde style that raise the question: is it actually love that is displayed in the image?

Towards the end of the nineteenth century in Europe, groups of artists known as Secessionists broke away from the formal teaching of academies to focus on more experimental approaches to art. Klimt was part of the Viennese Secession, but resigned along with several colleagues to set up the independent 'Kunstschau' (Art Show) in Vienna in 1908. The art was heavily criticised, and the show was a financial disaster for its organisers, but for one bright spot – *The Kiss*, in its debut appearance, was recognised as a masterpiece and was purchased by the Austrian government in the national interest.

At first glance of the painting the impression is given of the man dominating his companion, and it has been suggested that the figures are Klimt himself and his long-time partner Emilie Flöge, merging together. But a tour of the piece finds much playful symbolism and ambiguity to keep us as wrapped up in the kiss as the couple encased in gold, and to keep questioning the nature of the scene. As we look closer at her feet, we release she is kneeling while he apparently is standing up – if she were to stand too, she would tower over him.

Notice also the gold streamers that run away beneath her, which could be stylised tresses of longer hair. The Symobolists liked to portray *femmes fatales* with supernaturally

Klimt's Fulfilment *(1905-9), a preparatory design for the decoration of the interior of Stocklet Palace, Brussels, Belgium.*

long hair, ensnaring their male companions like spiders. With the man's face obscured our focus is directed to the woman, with her eyes closed in what is presumably romantic bliss. But critics have also pointed to the morbid undertones of her pale skin, and the fact that her head is tilted horizontally back, reminiscent of the paintings of decapitated heads that were so popular in Symbolist art at the time. Could this scene, then, have more in common with the Pierre Charles Comte 1849 painting of the post-mortem coronation of Inês de Castro (page 84)? Klimt left behind no explanation of the scene, and so the secrets of *The Kiss* remain its own, wrapped in its gold cocoon.

The Kiss Through the Ages

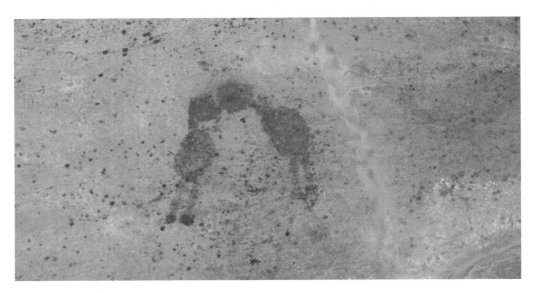

Above: The oldest depiction of a kiss: a 12,000-year-old cave painting apparently of a couple kissing, at the Pedra Furada archaeological site in the Serra da Capivara National Park, Brazil.

Above: A tondo (circular artwork) of an ancient Greek cup, showing a same-sex kiss between an older erastes *(lover) and his younger* eromenos *(beloved), c.480 BC.*

Right: A nude couple kiss on a bed in this Old Babylonian clay model that was moulded and fired over 3,800 years ago, in c.1800 BC.

Above: In Giotto's masterpiece fresco The Arrest of Christ (The Kiss of Judas) *(1304-06), Judas reaches up and plants his traitor's kiss on Christ, as they are surrounded by the commotion of followers and enemies. Part of the* Cycle of the Life of Christ *frescoes painted by Giotto at the Scrovegni Chapel, Padua, Italy.*

Above: François Boucher's *(1703-70)* Hercules and Omphale *(1735), a surprisingly rare example of a romantic kiss in Renaissance art. Sold into slavery to Queen Omphale of Ludia, Hercules falls for her enchantment, and loses his desire to continue performing his tasks.*

Left: Psyche Revived by Cupid's Kiss *(1787-93), by the greatest sculptor of the European Neoclassical period, Antonio Canova (1757-1822). The Venetian artist's unparalleled skill of simulating flesh from stone is clear in this masterpiece of mythological love, showing the god Cupid awakening Psyche.*

Left: Marc Chagall (1887-1985) referred to love as the 'primary colour' of his paintings. For him the muse came in form of the love of his life, Bella, whom he met as a teenager and eventually married in 1915, despite the objections of her parents. Chagall painted The Birthday *just a few weeks before the couple were due to marry, capturing the dizzying sense of joy in the tumbling, dreamlike scene.*

Above Left: The Kiss *(1859) by the Italian artist Francesco Hayez (1791-1881). In the style of Italian Romanticism, a couple from the Middle Ages are shown in a passionate embrace. Shadows lurk around them – it's thought the painting symbolises young Italian soldiers of Hayez's time kissing their loved ones goodbye to fight for Italy against the Austro-Hungarian Empire.*

Above Right: In another of the most iconic images of love in the history of art, married Francesca da Rimini and her lover embrace in Rodin's The Kiss *(1882-9), before they, as Dante tells us in the* Inferno, *are condemned to hell for their sinful romance. Rodin originally planned to incorporate the couple into his Gates of Hell sculpture, but the public response was so great to* The Kiss *that he left the pair as their own artwork.*

Left: René Magritte's (1898-1967) extraordinary The Lovers, *painted in Paris in 1928. The rather disturbing painting subverts the clichéd kiss, denying us the pleasure of seeing the faces as the lovers touch. It could draw on Magritte's experience as a teenager when his mother drowned, with her nightgown covering her face.*

Below: Kiss at South Kensington Station (2013), by the author, a Doisneau devotee.

Above: The Kiss by the Hôtel de Ville *(1950) by Robert Doisneau. The kiss caught at the corner of rue du Renard and rue de Rivoli is not as authentic as it was long assumed – the couple were actors and friends of Doisneau, who used them as subjects to avoid complex legal issues with strangers' image rights. There was no posing involved, however, as Doisneau simply followed his friends, snapping pictures as they strode around town.*

Frida Kahlo's Diego in My Thoughts (1943) *and the Art of Obsession*

For the first major exhibition of Frida Kahlo's work, at the Julien Lévy Gallery in New York in 1938, an accompanying essay was commissioned in which the founder of surrealism André Breton hailed her work as 'a ribbon around a bomb' and claimed her as a self-formed surrealist. As much as Kahlo (1907-54) enjoyed the appreciation of her work, she disagreed with the label, and resisted it throughout her career. 'They thought I was a surrealist but I wasn't. I never painted dreams. I painted my own reality.'

Kahlo once wrote of there having been two great accidents in her life. The first occurred on 17 September 1925, when Kahlo and her boyfriend, Arias, were on a bus that was struck by an electric tram. An iron handrail punctured her pelvis, abdomen and uterus, 'the way a sword pierces a bull', she wrote later. The handrail was then wrenched from her body by Arias and some other passengers, to her agony. Her spine was broken in three places, her right leg broken in eleven places (it would eventually be amputated in 1953, a year before her death).

That was the first terrible accident. 'The other,' she wrote, 'was Diego. Diego was by far the worst.' The notorious marriage of Frida Kahlo and the painter Diego Rivera was passionate, volatile, blissful, tragic; riddled with extra-marital affairs and yet incurably underpinned by a deep and essential mutual love. 'Your word travels the entirety of space and reaches my cells which are my stars,' she wrote in a love letter to her husband, 'then goes to yours which are my light.'

Kahlo's *Self-portrait as a Tehuana*, also titled *Diego in My Thoughts* and *Thinking of Diego*, works to represent the complexity and obsession in her relationship with Diego, but also the contradictions inherent in so many loving relationships. The man she loved

returned the affection yet would also indulge a desire to punish her. 'If I ever loved a woman, the more I loved her, the more I wanted to hurt her,' wrote Diego. 'Frida was only the most obvious victim of this disgusting trait.' And yet still she cannot help but obsess over him.

Kahlo began painting the self-portrait in August 1940 when she and Diego finally divorced, after his repeated betrayals of affairs with other women. This included a fling with her sister, Cristina, in 1935, which devastated Kahlo. In response she cut off all her hair and began the painting *Memory (The Heart)*, (see overleaf), which she completed two years later. In this self-portrait her eyes overflow with tears of grief, with an empty space where her heart should be, run through with an arrow-like stake, while the heart lies pummelled and bleeding at her feet. She stands with one foot on the blood-stained ground and the other on a dark beckoning sea, helpless without hands.

In *Self-portrait as a Tehuana*, Kahlo is more dignified, cauterised by Diego's infidelities, but paints his portrait on her forehead, an obsession she realises she will never obtain. She portrays herself with dignity, proudly and resiliently dressed in the traditional Mexican Tehuana costume of her ancestors, originating with the Zapotec civilisation. (Tehuana society is traditionally egalitarian – women do not rely

on the men as providers and have had just as many social and economic freedoms as men, able to remain single, divorce or marry as they please.)

By the time Kahlo finished the self-portrait in 1943, she and Diego had remarried. Her injuries would worsen and torture her throughout her life – her friend Andrés Henestrosa (1906-2008) once said of her that she 'lived dying'. By the mid-1940s, Kahlo's back pain was such that she could neither sit nor stand, and so in June 1945 she went to New York for an operation to fuse a bone graft and steel support to her spine, in order to straighten it. It was a procedure on which all her hopes were pinned, and it failed. She died on 13 July 1954, which Diego described as 'the most tragic day of my life. I had lost my beloved Frida forever. Too late now I realized that the most wonderful part of my life had been my love for Frida.'

Opposite: Kahlo's Memory (The Heart), *1937.*

Above: Between 1940 and 1954, to treat her worsening spinal issues Frida Kahlo wore twenty-eight different supportive corsets, some made from steel, some leather and some plaster, which she would decorate to transform into works of art.

The Surprising History of the Dating App

Ours is the era of the digital dating app, which according to one extensive survey by the Statistic Brain Research Institute of America is instrumental in the formation of one in five modern relationships, and a little more than one in six marriages. Dating apps are so successful, in fact, that it isn't just humans using them. Since 2017 the Apenheul primate park in Apeldoorn, a province of the Netherlands, has conducted what it calls 'Tinder for orangutans', allowing its female orangutans to browse digital profiles of potential mates from an international great ape breeding programme.[1]

In the self-publicising profiles of dating apps, we can trace an ancestry that goes back through the VCR dating services that began in the 1970s (in which one recorded a dating profile to camera), the 'lonely hearts' columns of newspapers earlier in the same century, all the way back to the early eighteenth century and the matrimonial advertisement.

The story goes that one of the earliest such advertisements ever placed in a newspaper was written by an Englishwoman named Helen Morrison in 1727, in the *Manchester Weekly Journal*. In a short paragraph, she simply appealed for a pleasant man to share life with. Such a public plea was unheard of. Controversy ensued, the advertisement was reported, and the city's mayor ordered that Helen be committed to a mental institution for a month. For centuries shame and stigma would be associated with matrimonial advertisements, the later 'personal ads', and even to a lesser degree the embarrassment of early internet dating. And this, I think, is what makes these little communiqués such a poignant read: that despite the shame, the appeals were made regardless.

As we know all too well from modern politics not everyone has the ability to feel embarrassment. Take the grand matrimonial advertisement shown here, which is unusual – given the more common desire for anonymity – in that it is both signed and illustrated with a portrait. Sir John Dinely, 5th Baronet (1729-1809), was a notorious eccentric known for spending the remainder of his family fortune, matching the wastefulness of his twin brother Edward who died insane and unmarried at the age of thirty-two, and of their father who was hanged for the murder of his own elder brother in 1741. Sir John would often be seen among the crowds of large public events at Windsor, dressed in a magnificent but filthy George II-era outfit of embroidered coat, silk waistcoat and stockings, relentlessly in pursuit of his one obsession: finding a wife.

All he needed to regain his family's fortune, he believed, was an initial sum to engage good legal assistance. His plan was to acquire this investment through marriage. 'He had a wonderful discrimination in avoiding the tittering girls with whose faces he was familiar,' wrote a contemporary journalist in *Penny Magazine*. 'But perchance some buxom matron or timid maiden who had seen him for the first time gazed upon the apparition with

---

1 The trick, apparently, is in constructing a digital tablet strong enough to withstand the orangutans' enthusiastic tapping. A steel-reinforced frame solved the problem, until one female ape nicknamed by her keepers 'Demolition Woman' got a hold of it.

TO THE
FAIR LADIES OF GREAT BRITAIN,
OLD, or YOUNG.

Sir John DINELY, Baronet, having it in his power to offer to any Lady who may be inclined to enter into the sacred and all-soothing state of Matrimony, not only the Title of LADY, but a FORTUNE of THREE HUNDRED THOUSAND POUNDS, besides the very great probability of succeeding to a CORONET,—condescends thus publicly to tender his hand to such Ladies as are qualified* to accept his MARRIAGE OFFER upon the terms stipulated in his Advertisement in the Morning Advertiser of the 4th of Jan. last.

Sir John is aware that some few, prejudiced by etiquette, may smile at his mode of address;—let them laugh:—he has once experienced its comfortable effects, and will not be dissuaded from giving it a decided preference to the tedious forms of fashionable routine.

All the objections that can possibly be urged against this maxim,—"that it is equally incumbent on the Ladies, as on the Gentlemen, boldly to advance in a candid and liberal manner in matrimonial negociations," are merely chimerical: the advantages in favor of it, are great and many. By pursuing this principle, the sickly Damsel who has long pined in secret, may recover her health. The woe-begone Widow, whose weeds are an almost insupportable load, may be relieved from her burthen; and, the sweet blooming Miss of Sixteen, to whom the trammels of a boarding school are quite intolerable, may be raised to Liberty and Love!!! Let me entreat you, therefore, my angelic Fair, ingenuously to unbosom your sentiments,

nor trust to dangerous delay, for I am resolved to give her the Preference who is most explicit and most expeditious.

* As many Ladies may not have seen the Advertisement above referred to, Sir John thinks it necessary to explain what is meant by the word "QUALIFIED";—and he trusts no person will be offended at his frankness: He therefore, premises that previous to his entering upon a Treaty of Marriage with any Lady, he must be assured of her being possessed of such of the following Sums, as is required according to her age and condition; viz. Those under Twenty-one, only Three Hundred Pounds;—those from Twenty-one to Thirty, Five Hundred; and from Thirty to Forty, Six Hundred. All Spinsters turned of that age, must be treated with according to circumstances; and, probably few will be eligible with less than a Thousand. However, Widows under Forty-five will have such Abatement as personal Charms and accomplishments entitle them to expect.

These several sums, are mere trifles, compared with what Sir John might reasonably demand, on account of his high and noble Descent, which may be seen in Nash's History of Worcestershire; and his Claims to the vast family estates known, by a Reference to JOHN WATTS, Esq. No. 34, Queen Ann Street, East, London.

JOHN DINELY.

P. S. Please to address your Letters, Post paid, to Sir John Dinely, Bart. Windsor Castle.

Pubd Feb. 16 1799 by C Knight Windsor.

THE COURTEOUS BARONET
OR THE WINDSOR ADVERTISER

How happy will a Lady be
To have a little Baronet, to dandle on her Knee

I do hereby declare this New Edition of my last Address to the Ladies, to be a true Copy, and that Mr. C. Knight hath my Authority to publish the same as an Embellishment to my Portrait

Windsor Castle, October 23d, 1799.

John Dinely

Printed by C. Knight, Windsor.

THE ADVERTISEMENT FOR A WIFE.

surprise and curiosity. He approached. With the air of one bred in courts he made his most profound bow; and taking a printed paper from his pocket, reverently presented it and withdrew.' The advertisement shown on the previous page is an example of those that Sir John handed out and had printed in newspapers. He continued his search for a wife throughout his life. He died, having never married, at Windsor in November 1809, and the baronetcy became extinct.[2]

The Advertisement for a Wife *(1821) by Thomas Rowlandson, showing the hazards of an eligible bachelor making such an appeal in the newspapers.*

As Sir John had found, the practical benefits of marriage overrode the hesitancy with which one approached the commission of one's own matrimonial advert. One needn't be coy about it, as demonstrated by the recently widowed applicant who wrote in his advertisement in the *Dorset County Chronicle* of 23 August 1832: 'I do not want a second family. I want a woman to look after the pigs while I am out at work.' Others were upfront about different aspects. Any lady possessing 'good teeth, soft lips, sweet breath, with eyes …' was good enough for the author of a posting in the *Sheffield Independent* on 1 February 1866. 'A good magician and magnetic healer wishes to meet a little blond song-and-dance or elocution lady, from 20 to 30 years' ran another from the

---

2 Incidentally, on the subject of unique marriage postings, in Massachusetts the 17 September 1771 edition of the local *Essex Gazette* carried this bitter anti-marriage advertisement by a Josiah Woodbury, announcing that his wife had left him, and he was totally fine about it, happy even, he definitely wasn't devastated and didn't miss her at all: 'RAN AWAY from Josiah Woodbury, Cooper, his House Plague for 7 long years, Masury Old Moll, alias Trial of Vengeance. He that lost will never seek her; he that shall keep her, I will give two Bushels of Beans. I forewarn all Persons in Town and Country from trusting said Trial of Vengeance. I have hove all the old Shoes I can find for Joy; all my neighbours rejoice with me. A good riddance of bad Ware. Amen. JOSIAH WOODBURY.'

Right Top: Harmony before Matrimony, an 1805 caricature by James Gillray, a scene of blissful musical courtship that satirises the practice of teaching women a musical skill to attract a husband.

Right Bottom: Its partner cartoon Matrimonial Harmonics, in which the skill has lost its appeal after several years of marriage.

Minneapolis Star Tribune of 17 May 1903. 'If suited will make you a kind husband and nice home in the West; give height and weight in first letter.' 'A middle-aged gentleman, of forty' advertised in the *Bath Chronicle and Weekly Gazette* of Thursday 2 May 1850, wishing to 'most ardently meet with a lady who would accept the entire devotion of his hand and heart', with the addendum: 'N.B. He is bald, but will wear a wig if the lady wishes.' Advertisements by women seeking husbands could possess a noticeably more romantic tone: 'Widow, 44, Southerner, stranger, own home, West End, would like the hearthstone of her heart swept, and the cobwebs brushed away; matrimony' (*St Louis Post-Dispatch*, 16 April 1899). Expectations were kept realistic, though: 'A young girl, seventeen years of age, who knows how to make good soup, desires to marry someone, no matter who, and would not even object to a person with a broken leg. Address, Mdlle.---' (*Dundee Courier,* 13 April 1880).

If you were particularly unlucky, however, your matrimonial advertisement could lead to you being subjected to an early form of 'catfishing' (impersonation) by scammers, robbers, or even bored teenage boys, like the poor fellow reported on in the *Mayo Constitution* of 10 January 1831. After exchanging letters with a self-described attractive 'nymph of twenty-two', who

HARMONY *before* MATRIMONY.

MATRIMONIAL-HARMONICS.

boasted of a fortune of £200 and a wealthy grandmother nearing the end, our young hero eagerly requested a romantic meeting. An evening walk along the Royal Circle in Brighton was agreed. The date going well, he lunged for a kiss, but 'the bonnet of his fair *inamorata* fell off and was accompanied in its fall by a thundering "Damn, the bonnet!" from the "Lady". Our hero … beheld what before escaped his observation, a pair of huge Wellington boots in lieu of the delicate sandal or spruce half-boot. A loud horse-laugh from some wags in ambush accompanied the denouement, and the luckless lover hastened home completely cured of his *maladie d'amour*.'

Voyager *Golden Record – The Love Story that Left the Solar System*

Alone on its journey across the vast sea of interstellar space, having left behind our solar system in August 2012, is the probe *Voyager 1*. Launched on 5 September 1977 following the launch of its sister spacecraft *Voyager 2* on 20 August 1977, at the time of writing, *Voyager 1* is approximately 23,790,226,634 kilometres from Earth, speeding through the Ophiuchus (Serpent Bearer) Constellation. Composed of equipment to collect and transmit data of the wonders they explore, both craft also carry a 'message in a bottle': a gold record holding audio recordings and photographs representative of life on Earth. 'It was a chance to tell something about what life on earth was like to beings of a thousand million years from now,' said Ann Druyan, the creative director of NASA's Voyager Interstellar Message Project. 'If that didn't raise goosebumps then you'd have to be made of wood.'

The creation of the Golden Record was apportioned just $25,000 of the Voyager project's budget of $865 million. Druyan and the committee in charge of selecting its contents, chaired by the astronomer Carl Sagan, were given just six weeks to complete it. Druyan and Sagan worked closely at all hours to accomplish the gigantic task, fuelled by the knowledge that their work would be a beacon carried through space for the next thousand million years. Their interstellar 'mixtape' carries to its alien listeners all manner of human and

The Sounds of Earth, *otherwise known as the Golden Record, holding the story of Earth, created by NASA's Voyager Interstellar Message Project, headed by Carl Sagan and Ann Druyan, for the* Voyager *spacecraft.*

non-human experiences on Earth. Recordings of Bach, Mozart and Beethoven sit together with the 1959 rock song 'Johnny B Goode', as well as greetings voiced in the fifty-nine most used languages – and one non-human language, in a recording of the greetings of humpback whales. Sagan's son Nick greets alien life on behalf of all human children, and Sagan's own laugh is recorded. The sounds of waves and rain, bubbles, frogs, birds and dogs, along with the sounds of pulsars, trains, planes and cars fill the phonograph. 'It was a sacred undertaking,' said Druyan, 'because it was saying, "We want to be citizens of the cosmos, we want you to know about us."'

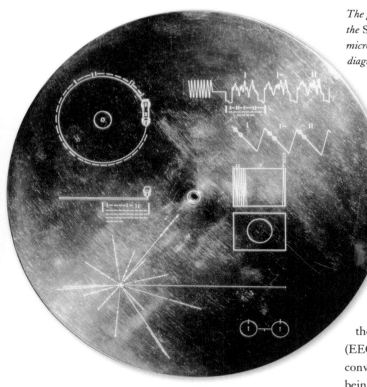

The gold aluminium cover designed to protect the Sounds of Earth *gold-plated records from micrometeorite bombardment, as well as carry a diagrammatic key explaining how to play the record.*

At about twenty minutes and fifty-one seconds into the golden phonograph recording there is a particularly strange sound, after the roar of a rocket lifting off, and a mother lovingly kissing and soothing a crying baby. For about a minute there is a stream of fireworks popping, bursting and crackling, a bit like a pyrotechnic New Year's Eve celebration. In fact, what we can hear is the sound of a mind in love. These are the brainwaves recorded for the project in an electroencephalogram (EEG) of Ann Druyan, following her idea to convert thought to sound, with the notion that beings of the distant future would be able to convert it back. Just two days earlier, Druyan had left a message on Sagan's answering machine, ecstatically reporting that she'd found the perfect piece of Chinese music to add to the recording, a 2,500-year-old composition called *Flowing Streams*. Sagan called her back, and the two had an hour-long conversation. By the time it was over, the pair, who had never had any personal discussion with each other, let alone so much as kissed, had declared their love to each other and Druyan had proposed marriage. She told NPR in an interview in 2010:

'We both hung up the phone, and I just screamed out loud. I remember it so well because it was this great, eureka moment. And then the phone rang, and it was Carl again, and he's like, "I just want to make sure

The Voyager 1 *Golden Record is prepared for installation on the spacecraft, 1977.*

Engineers secure the cover over the Voyager 1 *Golden Record.*

that really happened. We're getting married, right?" And I said, "Yep, we're getting married." He said, "OK, just wanted to make sure." And the spacecraft lifted off on August 20th, and August 22nd we told everyone involved. And we were together from that moment until his death in 1996, in December.'

Two days after their phone call, still buzzing with excitement, Druyan recorded the EEG at Bellevue Hospital in New York. 'My feelings as a 27-year-old woman, madly fallen in love, they're on that record. It's for ever. It'll be true 100 million years from now. For me *Voyager* is a kind of joy so powerful, it robs you of your fear of death.'

When Sagan died on 20 December 1996, Druyan wrote a note in his memory, revealing that the two had shared the philosophy that 'every single moment that we were alive and we were together was miraculous – not miraculous in the sense of inexplicable or supernatural. We knew we were beneficiaries of chance … That pure chance could be so generous and so kind … That we could find each other, in the vastness of space and the immensity of time … That we could be together for twenty years. That is something which sustains me and it's much more meaningful … The way he treated me and the way I treated him, the way we took care of each other and our family, while he lived. That is so much more important than the idea I will see him someday. I don't think I'll ever see Carl again. But I saw him. We saw each other. We found each other in the cosmos, and that was wonderful.'

Carl Sagan with his wife Ann Druyan in the 1990s.

Out into the universe sails their story, the brainwaves of a human in love etched into gold discs and strapped to the sides of spacecraft expected to still be travelling long after the human race has come to its end. Which is so neatly embodied by the sentiment with which Philip Larkin ends his poem 'An Arundel Tomb' mentioned previously in this book, written years before in 1956, after seeing the marble effigies of the medieval husband and wife lying beside each other with their hands joined, in Chichester Cathedral:

What will survive of us is love.

Select Bibliography

Armstrong, K. (2005) *A Short History of Myth*, Edinburgh: Canongate

Baynton-Williams, A. (2015) *The Curious Map Book*, London: British Library

Bloch, I. (1909) *The Sexual Life of Our Time in its Relations to Modern Civilization*, London: Rebman Ltd

Bondeson, J. (1997) *A Cabinet of Medical Curiosities*, London: I. B. Tauris Publishers

Budge, E. A. W. (1975) *Egyptian Religion: Ideas of the Afterlife in Ancient Egypt*, London: Routledge & Kegan Paul

Camille, M. (1998) *The Medieval Art of Love: Objects and Subjects of Desire*, London: Laurence King

Clarke, A. (2011) *Love Letters: 2000 Years of Romance*, London: British Library

Cocks, H. G. (2009) *Classified: The Secret History of the Personal Column*, London: Random House

Coontz, S. (2006) *Marriage, a History*, London: Penguin

Davies, O. (2009) *Grimoires: A History of Magic Books*, Oxford: Oxford University Press

Doyle, U. (ed.) (2019) *Love Letters of Great Men*, London: Macmillan

Fisher, H. (2017) *Anatomy of Love: A Natural History of Mating, Marriage, and Why We Stray*, New York: W.W. Norton

Ford, B. J. (1992) *Images of Science: A History of Scientific Illustration*, London: British Library

Gilbert, R. (2020) *The Very Secret Sex Lives of Medieval Women*, Coral Gables, FL: Mango

Gristwood, S. (2021) *The Tudors in Love: The Courtly Code Behind the Last Medieval Dynasty*, London: Oneworld

Haggard, H. W. (1913) *Devils, Drugs and Doctors*, London: Harper & Brothers

Harvey, K. (2021) *The Fires of Lust: Sex in the Middle Ages*, Padstow: TJ Books Ltd

Howgego, R. (2003-2013) *Encyclopedia of Exploration*, Sydney: Hordern House

Langhamer, C. (2013) *The English in Love: The Intimate Story of an Emotional Revolution*, Oxford: Oxford University Press

Lister, K. (2020) *A Curious History of Sex*, London: Unbound

Lovejoy, B. (2013) *Rest in Pieces: The Curious Fates of Famous Corpses*, New York: Simon & Schuster

McCarthy, C. (2022) *Love, Sex & Marriage in the Middle Ages*, Abingdon: Routledge

May, S. (2011) *Love: A History*, New Haven: Yale University Press

Munsinger, H. L. (2019) *The History of Marriage and Divorce: Everything You Need to Know*, Bloomington: Archway

Penner, B. (2009) *Newlyweds on Tour: Honeymooning in Nineteenth-Century America*, Durham, NH: University of New Hampshire Press

Pritchard, R. E. (2021) *Sex, Love and Marriage in the Elizabethan Age*, Philadelphia: Pen and Sword Books

Riddell, F. (2021) *Sex: Lessons From History*, London: Hodder & Stoughton

Ridley, G. (2011) *The Discovery of Jeanne Baret*, London: Random House

Roach, M. (2008) *Bonk: The Curious Coupling of Science and Sex*, New York: W.W. Norton & Company

Rose, D. (2010) *Sexually, I'm more of a Switzerland: Personal Ads from the London Review of Books*, London: Picador

De Rougemont, D. (1956) *Love in the Western World*, New York: Pantheon

Shaftesbury, P. (2018) *Love, Sex & Marriage: Relationship Tips From the Victorians*, London: Summersdale

Took, J. (2020) *Dante*, Princeton, NJ: Princeton University Press

Trafford, L. J. (2021) *Sex and Sexuality in Ancient Rome*, Philadelphia: Pen and Sword

Tucker, S. D. (2016) *Forgotten Science*, Stroud: Amberley Publishing

Usher, S. (ed.) (2020) *Letters of Note: Love*, London: British Library

Zuffi, S. (2008) *Love and the Erotic Art*, Milan: Mondadori

Index

Page numbers in *italics* refer to illustrations; page numbers followed by a 'n' refer to footnotes

Picture Credits

PP1, 3 Metropolitan Museum of Art; P9 Herzogliches Museum; P10 Sotheby's New York; P11 (left) Wellcome Collection; P11 (right) British Library; P12 (top) Rijksmuseum; P12 (bottom) Wellcome Collection; P13 Metropolitan Museum of Art; P14 Auckland Art Gallery Toi o Tamaki New Zealand; P15 Wellcome Collection; PP16-17 British Library; P18 Geni, wikipedia.co.uk; P20 Nessy Pic; P21 (left) Ramessos, Wikipedia.co.uk; P21 (right) Thilo Parg; P22 Nevit Dilmen; P23 Tilemahos Efthimiadis; P24 Babelstone; P25 (bottom) FAMSI.org; P26 (top right) ebay.co.uk; P26 (bottom) Metropolitan Museum of Art; P27 Metropolitan Museum of Art; PP28-29 www.uppsalaauktion.se; P30 Françoise Foliot; P32 Turp, AB. et al., *Gynecological Endocrinology*, 2017; P33 Royal Holloway College (London); P34 Osama Shukir Muhammed Amin FRCP (Glasg); P35 Yoav Dothan; P36 Metropolitan Museum of Art; P37 Metropolitan Museum of Art; P38 Ancient Peoples, Tumblr.com; P39 Jon Bodsworth; P40 Metropolitan Museum of Art; P41 Metropolitan Museum of Art; P43 Zhongguo gu dai shu hua jian ding zu; P48 Bengt Littorin; P49 Metropolitan Museum of Art; P52 Kim Traynor; P53 Fer.filol; P54 Heinrich Stürzl; P55 Marie-Lan Nguyen; P56 ArchaiOptix; P57 Carole Raddato; P59 Wellcome Collection; P60 (both images) Sailko, Wikipedia. co.uk; P61 (both images) Wellcome Collection; P62 (both images) Jean-Pierre Dalbera; P63 Bijaya2043; P64 Los Angeles County Museum of Art; P65 Library of Geneva; P66 Michel Wal; P67 Bodleian Library; P69 (top) Museo Larco, Peru; P70 National Museum of Denmark; P71 National Museum of Denmark; P72 National Museum of Wales; P73 National Portrait Gallery, London; P74 Rodw, Wikipedia.co.uk; P75 National Museum of Wales; P78 Walker Art Gallery, Liverpool; P79 (top) Marie-Lan Nguyen; P79 (bottom) Metropolitan Museum of Art; P81 National Library of France; P82 French National Library; PP84-85 Scailyna; PP86-87 SaraPCNeves; P88 Matthew T. Rader; P89 Victoria and Albert Museum; P90 William Donelson; P91 Arian Zwegers; P92 Ziegler175, Wikipedia.co.uk; P93 Diliff, Wikipedia.co.uk; P94 Museum Fine Arts, Boston; P95 (top) Metropolitan Museum of Art; P95 (bottom) Sailko; P96 (left) Metropolitan Museum of Art; P96 (right) Photo by Tom Oates; P97 Frank Janssen; P98 thehistoryblog.com; P99 (top left) Penn Museum; P99 (bottom left) Paolo Terzi; P99 (right) Dagmar Hollmann; P101 National Gallery; P102 National Gallery; P103 The Yorck Project; P105 Royal Library of Copenhagen; P106 Bavarian State Library, Munich; P107 Hermitage; PP108-113 Metropolitan Museum of Art; P114 (top) State Library of Württemberg; P114 (bottom) French National Library; P116 (top) Wellcome Collection; P116 (bottom left) Metropolitan Museum of Art; P116 (bottom right) French National Library; P117 (top left) Los Angeles County Museum of Art; P117 (top middle) Metropolitan Museum of Art; P117 (top right) Daniel Ullrich; P117 (bottom right) Wikipedia.co.uk; P118 History and Art Collection/Alamy Stock Photo; P120 British Library; P121 Flominator, Wikipedia.co.uk; P122 British Library; P123 British Library; P124 (top) Metropolitan Museum of Art; P124 (bottom) Universitätsbibliothek Heidelberg; P125 British Library; P126 The J. Paul Getty Museum, Los Angeles; P127 Metropolitan Museum of Art; P128 (both images) National Library of France; P129 British Library; P130 British Library; P131 Wikipedia.co.uk; P132 Museum der bildenden Künste; P134 British Library; P135 Wellcome Collection; P137 Wellcome Collection; P139 Wellcome Collection; P140 Simon Speed; P141 Cooper Hewitt Museum; P142 BoolaBoola2, Wikipedia. co.uk; PP143-144 (all images) Sydney Living Museums; P146 National Trust/Christopher Warleigh-Lack; P147 Victoria and Albert Museum; P148 Cornell University; P149 Boston Public Library; PP150-151 Cornell University Library; P154 Metropolitan Museum of Art; P155 (both images) Courtesy of David Western, www.davidwesternlovespoons.com; P156 (top left) Jerry 'Woody', Wikipedia.co.uk; P156 (bottom) Metropolitan Museum of Art; P157 Christie's; P158 (top) Smithsonian American Art Museum; P158 (top, top right) Smithsonian American Art Museum; P158 (middle right, bottom right, left middle) Metropolitan Museum of Art; P159 (top) National Museum of Sweden; P159 (top right) Lubomirski Museum; P159 (bottom right) Philadelphia Museum of Art; P159 (bottom left) National Museum of Sweden; P159 (middle left) National Galleries; P160 British Library; P161 British Library; P162 British Library; P163 British Library; PP164–165 British Library; PP167-169 Alamy Stock Photo; P170 Herbier Muséum, Paris; PP172-173 Barry Lawrence Ruderman Antique Maps; P175 (left) Metropolitan Museum of Art; P175 (right) Afrika Museum, Berg en Dal; P176 Afrika Museum, Berg en Dal; P177 Afrika Museum, Berg en Dal; P179 (top) British Library; P179 (bottom) wikipedia.co.uk; P182 Library of Congress; P183 National Library of France; P184 Library of Congress; P187 Philadelphia Museum of Art; PP188-189 Metropolitan

Museum of Art; P190 Colleter R, Dedouit F, Duchesne S, Mokrane F-Z, Gendrot V, Gérard P, et al.; P191 British Library; P192 Balliol College, Oxford; P193 Pitt Rivers Museum; P194 Courtesy of St Andrews Library; P195 (right) Wellcome Collection; P196 Metropolitan Museum of Art; P197 Massachusetts Historical Society; P198 Museum of Fine Arts, Boston; P199 Wellcome Collection; P200 British Museum; P201 Dnalor 01, Wikipedia.co.uk; P202 British Library; P205 Aflo Co. Ltd./Alamy Stock Photo; P207 Wolfgang Adler; P208 Andriy Makukha; P209 University of Heidelberg; P210 Wikipedia.co.uk; PP212-215 Courtesy of Maggs Bros. Ltd. Rare Books and Manuscripts, London; P216 New York Public Library; P217 Tobias Schrödel; P218 (both images) Tobias Schrödel; P219 (bottom) Tobias Schrödel; P220 (both images) Tobias Schrödel; PP223-225 (224, top) Smithsonian; P224 (bottom) Keystone Press; P226 MAK – Museum of Applied Arts, Vienna; P227 Belvedere Museum Vienna; P228 (top) Vitor 1234, Wikipedia.co.uk; P228 (bottom right) British Museum; P228 (bottom left) Marie-Lan Nguyen, Wikipedia.co.uk; P229 (top left) Geoff Wren, Wikipedia.co.uk; P229 (top right) Pushkin State Museum of Fine Art; P229 (bottom) Jean-Pol Grandmont; P230 (top) The Museum of Modern Art, New York/Scala, Florence; P230 (bottom left) Pinacoteca di Brera, Milan; P230 (bottom right) Tylwyth Eldar; P231 (top) MOMA; P231 (bottom left) Robert DOISNEAU/Gamma-Rapho/Getty Images; P233 GRANGER - Historical Picture Archive/Alamy Stock Photo; P234 Archivart/Alamy Stock Photo; P235 Betty Johnson/Alamy Stock Photo; P239 Library of Congress; PP240-242 (all images) NASA/JPL-Caltech; P243 colaimages/Alamy Stock Photo.

All other images are the author's own or public domain.

Every effort has been made to find and credit the copyright holders of images in this book. We will be pleased to rectify any errors or omissions in future editions.

Front cover: A section of The Garden of Earthly Delights by Hieronymus Bosch

Acknowledgements

I would like to express my deep appreciation to all who provided such indispensable help in the creation of this book: to Charlie Campbell at Greyhound Literary; to Ian Marshall; to Alison MacDonald at Simon & Schuster UK; to Laura Nickoll and Keith Williams for yet another beautiful design, and to John English. I'm especially grateful to Tobias Schrödel for so generously providing and allowing the reproduction of items from his collection of cryptic postcards, and to Ed Maggs at Maggs Bros for so kindly allowing the reproduction of images of the Henry Hilditch Bulkeley-Johnson manuscript and for sharing his wonderful research. With many thanks to my family for all their support, and to Alex and Alexi Anstey, Matt, Gemma, Charlie and Wren Troughton, Kate Awad, Katherine Anstey, Georgie Hallett, Thea Lees, and Ruth Millington; and to John Lloyd, Dan Schreiber, Andy Hunter Murray, and Jason Hazeley. My love to all.

First published in Great Britain by Simon & Schuster UK Ltd, 2023

Copyright © 2023 by Edward Brooke-Hitching

Editorial Director: Alison MacDonald
Project Editor: Laura Nickoll
Design: Keith Williams, sprout.uk.com

1 3 5 7 9 10 8 6 4 2

Simon & Schuster UK Ltd
1st Floor
222 Gray's Inn Road
London WC1X 8HB

www.simonandschuster.co.uk

Simon & Schuster Australia,
Sydney
www.simonandschuster.com.au

Simon & Schuster India,
New Delhi
www.simonandschuster.co.in

The author and publishers have made all reasonable efforts to contact copyright-holders for permission, and
apologise for any omissions or errors in the form of credits given. Corrections may be made to future printings.

A CIP catalogue record for this book is available from the British Library

Hardback ISBN: 978-1-3985-2271-8
Ebook ISBN: 978-1-3985-2272-5

Printed in Dubai

MIX
Paper | Supporting
responsible forestry
FSC® C004800
FSC
www.fsc.org

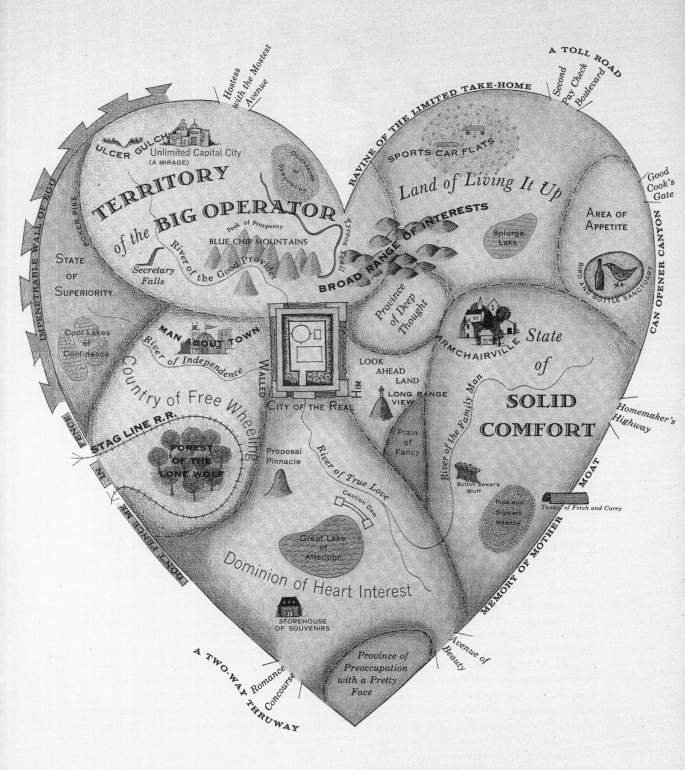

GEOGRAPHICAL GUIDE TO A
MAN'S HEART
with obstacles and entrances clearly marked